Thomas Pownall

A memorial, most humbly addressed to the sovereigns of Europe,

On the present state of affairs, between the Old and New World

Thomas Pownall

A memorial, most humbly addressed to the sovereigns of Europe,
On the present state of affairs, between the Old and New World

ISBN/EAN: 9783337717674

Printed in Europe, USA, Canada, Australia, Japan

Cover: Foto ©ninafisch / pixelio.de

More available books at **www.hansebooks.com**

A

MEMORIAL,

MOST HUMBLY ADDRESSED

TO THE

SOVEREIGNS of EUROPE,

ON THE

PRESENT STATE of AFFAIRS,

BETWEEN THE

OLD AND NEW WORLD.

By T. POWNALL,

Late Governor, Captain-General, Vice-Admiral, &c. of the Provinces, now STATES, Massachusetts-Bay and South-Carolina; and Lieutenant-Governor of New-Jersey.

A NEW EDITION.

LONDON:

Printed for J. DEBRETT, (Successor to Mr. Almon,) Opposite Burlington House, Piccadilly.

[Price Half a Crown.]

PREFACE.

THE Memorial which I herewith fend you, was written by a Friend of mine, who is lately dead. It is of no confequence to the Public to be informed who he was. What he was, and of what fpirit, will appear by his Writings. A decifive misfortune in his perfonal relations had determined him to quit Europe, and to fettle in America: He had arranged his affairs to that end; and, although from the troubles which, in the interval of his preparations, arofe in America, he fufpended his actual fettlement in that Country; yet he fo far quitted Europe as to go and refide in the Azores or Weftern Ifles, devoting himfelf to that ftudy and contemplation
which

which was best suited to console him under his misfortunes, and to reconcile him to the sacrifice which he was about to make of every thing that remained to him of what the World holds most dear. I had the happiness of corresponding with him while he lived there, and I received this from him, with leave (if ever a time should arrive, in which I should think it might be of use) to publish it, on this condition, that I would write " something of a Preface
" to it. I do not," (*says he,) " like the
" Roman Statesman, say, *Orna me.* Leave
" me to oblivion, and in peace; for that is
" all I now seek. I am persuaded that the
" matter of facts, as the Memorial states
" it, and that the present combination of
" events, as the Memorial describes it, is
" *true:* That the consequences which I point
" out, as flowing from them, are *probable:*
" And that the conduct which I describe as
" that with which these things should be
" met, is the best wisdom for the Sovereigns
" of Europe, by which they can promote
" the

* In a letter dated *Nov.* 1778, *Ponta del Gada* in *St. Michael's.*

" the interest of their States, or the happi-
" ness of their People. * If the events do
" not come forward *at this period* as I sup-
" pose, or just *in the series of procession* as my
" reasoning hath attempted to draw the line,
" that is nothing to the age of the world,
" nor to the growing system of a state. The
" thing, therefore, which I ask of you, is,
"* to show how the general reasoning on the
" general train of events, applies to the cir-
" cumstances of the time whenever you shall
" publish it: And that you will give it (in
" French, or in any other language gene-
" rally understood) such a fashionable dress,
" such as that the world may receive it
" and understand it. Also, I wish that it
" may be understood how sensible I am
" that an *Apology* is necessary for my pre-
" suming to address a Memorial to Sove-
" reigns, on a subject in which they must
" be supposed to be perfectly informed, and
" in which your Friend (it may be sup-
" posed) can have so little practical informa-
" tion.

* They have, however, come forward at this period, 1783; and exactly in the series of procession as I drew the line.

" tion. Although, in what I am going to
" say, I shall shew no great art or addrefs,
" nor obferve that conduct which would be
" likely to recommend this Memorial to the
" great world; yet, for truth's fake, I will
" fay it, That I have always found that the
" Sovereigns, as far as they are informed, and
" are in circumftances to exert themfelves,
" have the intereft and profperity of their
" fubjects, the welfare and happinefs of
" mankind, more at heart, than it ever
" enters into the heads or hearts of their
" Minifters to conceive. It is for that rea-
" fon that I have prefumed to addrefs them.
" I will fet the great Henry of France at
" the head of the firft lift: One has heard
" of a Sully, a Fleury, a Clarendon, a
" Somers, a De Witt, a Franklin; and for
" the common good of mankind one would
" hope, that fuch men, in all countries
" where they can act, may never be want-
" ing to continue this other lift."

Although this my Preface will be formed chiefly by extracts from my Friend's letters,
who

who can beſt explain his own views, and which, without the parade of Authoriſm, are moſt fairly explained in thoſe private ſentiments: Yet, I doubt whether it may not be neceſſary to ſay, that though he here appears as an abſtracted Philoſopher, yet he was not unpracticed in the buſineſs of Government, nor uninformed by experience in a knowledge of the nature of the European Settlements in America. His life was a compound of buſineſs and frivolity *abroad:* He was a Philoſopher *at home*; and always, what may be very properly expreſſed, *very much at home.* He was conſcious that he thought very differently from the generality of mankind on thoſe ſubjects; and uſed while in Europe frequently to lament how little he was underſtood on the ſubject matter of this buſineſs. In a letter dated from the ſame place, in *March* 1779, he ſays, " When I look back, and compare my " opinions with events which ſeem to have " confirmed them, and yet ſee how little " effect theſe opinions have had, even when " called for, and when duly explained, by
" facts

" facts, in their proper place, I am at
" length convinced, that I have not the
" talent of so arranging, and of so explain-
" ing things, which I am sure are facts and
" truths, as to demonstrate them to others.
" That mind, whose faculties are most rea-
" dily exerted in the search of truth, is sel-
" dom habile and efficient in the demonstra-
" tion of it. This, therefore, will be the
" last Paper which I shall ever write on this
" side the world, on this subject. So little
" (if I am not too vain in a reference to my
" own ideas) was this subject compre-
" hended, so little did it seem interesting,
" so little was it relished, when I was in
" Europe, that I scarce ever talked of it in
" real earnest: And, although this with-
" drawn place may seem best suited for
" contemplation; yet I feel here the want
" of that correspondence and conversation,
" which elicites, and brings forward into
" effect, the power of reasoning, better
" than the closest and most intense study
" ever did. *Nec quenquam habeo quocum fa-*
" *miliariter de hujus modi rebus colloqui pos-*
" *sim;*

"*fim; ut ne faltem explicem & exacuam.*
"And I own I have my apprehensions that
"I may prove to be as *visionary,* as the
"world, I know, *will think me.*" Whether the world will be of opinion with my Friend's apprehensions or not, that this Memorial is visionary; you receive it, Mr. Almon, just as I received it. It appears to me to be founded in fact; to be plain and intelligible, is what I understand; and what therefore, I think, any other may very well understand. I hope, that, little as this Memorial is in its bulk, indeed not enough to make a book; it will neither be sold or read as a pamphlet *laxa cervice.* There is nothing in it to amuse such readers. If the matter which it contains, does not attract and engage the serious attention of serious men of business, it is neither worth your printing, nor their purchasing.

I differ from my Friend, and think it best that it should appear first in its own dress and language; I therefore send it to you, to print off an edition of it. I shall have

it

it tranflated afterward into a language that the generality of the world underftands, becaufe I think, that the matter which it contains, is of great importance to the States of Europe in general, as well as to England and America in a more particular manner.

 I am,

  Sir,

   Your Humble Servant,

    * * * * *

     Editor.

Paris, Jan. 25, 1780.

A

MEMORIAL, &c.

THAT NASCENT CRISIS,* which at the end of the laſt war " opened a a new channel of buſineſs, *and brought into operation a new concatenation of powers, both political and commercial,*" is now, at the beginning of this preſent war, come forward into birth, in perfect and eſtabliſhed ſyſtem. " *The ſpirit of commerce hath become a leading and predominant power*," it hath formed throughout North-America, and hath extended to Europe the baſis of a new commercial ſyſtem. " THE RISE AND FORMING OF THAT SYSTEM WAS WHAT PRECISELY CONSTITUTED THE CRISIS OF THAT TIME." It was ſeen by men who knew

how

---

* This quaint expreſſion, and the following paſſages, are taken from Governor Pownall's book on the Britiſh Colonies, firſt publiſhed in the year 1764.

how to profit of the knowledge; those who should have profitted would not see that "THAT ONE GENERAL COMPOSITE INTEREST" so formed, and so acting under the same laws, and by the same spirit of *attraction* which pervades all nature, must necessarily, in the procession of its power, have "A ONE COMMON CENTER OF GRAVITY AND UNION." There was, at that time, a State in Europe within whose dominions *that center* lay, coinciding nearly with the center of its own proper *political* system, and making even a part of its *natural* system. The operations of this composite system took a course almost in the very direction of the line of the natural movements of that State. The basis of a *great marine dominion* was laid by Nature, and the God of Nature offered that dominion to the only Power with which the spirit of liberty then dwelt. But the Government of that State, being wise in its own conceit, not only above, but against those things which existed, rejected Nature and would none of her ways; despised the wisdom of that

Providence

Providence which had established her. The spirit of attraction which Nature actuates was held to be a vision; and THAT STATE OF UNION, which the hand of God held forth, was blasphemed as folly. The Ministers of that country said to Repulsion, Thou shalt guide *our spirit*; to Distraction, Thou shalt be our wisdom. This spirit of Repulsion, this wisdom of Distraction, hath wrought the natural effect, dissolution. They have not only lost for ever the dominion which they might have wrought their nation up to, but the external parts of the Empire are one after another falling off, and it will be once more reduced to its insular existence.

On the other hand, *this new system* of power, united in and moving round its own proper center " *had dissolved the effect of all artificial* repulsions which force would create, and hath *formed those natural connections by and under* which its actual interest exists." Founded in Nature it is growing, by accelerated motions, and accumulated accretion of parts, into an independent, organized being, a great and powerful

powerful empire. *It has taken its equal station with the nations* upon earth.

Video solem orientem in occidente.

North-America is become a new *primary planet* in the system of the world, which while it takes its own course, in its own orbit, must have effect on the orbit of every other planet, and shift the common center of gravity of the whole system of the European world.

North-America is *de facto* AN INDEPENDENT POWER *which has taken its equal station with other powers*, and must be so *de jure*. The politicians of the Governments of Europe may reason or negociate upon this idea, as a matter *sub lite*. The powers of those Governments may fight about it as a new Power coming into establishment; such negociations, and such wars, are of no consequence either to the right or the fact. It would be just as wise, and just as effectual, if they were to go to war to decide, or set on foot negociations to settle, to whom for the future the sovereignty of the moon should belong. The moon hath been long common to them all, and they may

may all in their turns profit of her reflected light. The independence of America is fixed as fate; she is mistress of her own fortune;---knows that she is so, and will actuate that power which she feels she hath, so as to establish her own system, and to change the system of Europe.

I will not lose time, in an uselefs waste of words, by attempting to prove the existence of this fact. The rapid progress of events at this crisis will not wait for such trifling. The only thing which can be useful to the world is, to examine what the precise change of system is; what will be the general consequence of such change; and with what spirit, and by what conduct the advancing state of things should be met.

If the Powers of Europe will view the state of things *as they do really exist*, and will treat them *as being what they are*, the lives of thousands may be spared; the happiness of millions may be secured; and, the peace of the whole world preserved. If they will not, they will be plunged into a sea of troubles, a sea of blood, fathom-
less

less and boundless. The war that has begun to rage betwixt Britain, France, and Spain, which is almost gorged betwixt Britain and America, will extend itself to all the maritime, and most likely, afterwards, to all the inland powers of Europe: and like the *thirty years war* of the sixteenth and seventeenth centuries, will not end, but as that did, by a new and general resettlement of powers and interests, according to the new spirit of the new system which hath taken place. Why may not all this be done by a Congress of all the Powers before, as well as after war? If the Powers of the present world fought for dominion by extirpation, then war is the proper engine: but if they war in order to treat for settlements of power, as has been long the system of Europe, then is war a wanton, clumsey, useless cruelty. The final issue of the contest in the final settlement of power at a peace, is seldom (I think never) in proportion to the success of arms. It depends upon the interposition of parties, who have not, perhaps, meddled with the war, but who come to the treaty for

for peace. This interpofition, brought forward by intrigue, moſt commonly with the aid of jealoufy, doth counteract by negociation the envied effects of arms. If thofe who govern in Europe will look back to former wars, and will confider the views with which fuch were undertaken, will obferve the progrefs which they made, and the iſſue in which they terminated. If they will examine the various fyſtems planned for the enlargement of dominion, and the various ſtruggles under thofe plans, which have agitated their corner of the world, and will weigh the effect of thefe with the various forms of oppofition which hath been made to, and hath arreſted their progrefs, they will find, that negociation, and not war, determined thefe points.

The Britons have been *primeures in politics*, they have forced and brought forward the prefent rifing fyſtem into event and eſtabliſhment before its natural feafon. They might, with that addrefs which principles of truth and benevolence, deriving through common fenfe, direct, have fecured the attachment, and retained *the filial obedience*

obedience of their plantations for years to come (as the Spaniards with their caution will do;) but it was unfortunately for them, a principal part of the miserable, baseless plan of their inexperienced advisers, *the confidential counsellors* (in a general proposed reform of their King's government) to reform the constitutions of their American establishments. Although they could not be ignorant, although they were not uninformed, that the course of this reform must lead to war, yet having settled in their own minds an over-weening idea of the force of arms, they thought it *no bad move,* if they should (like giving check-mate at chess) force the Americans to have recourse to arms. Conquest, of which they made themselves sure, and settlements in consequence of such conquest, in which they would not suspect any other Power could interfere, would give them the proper right and proper power of altering the establishments, and of giving them just what constitutions they thought fit; such as that given to Quebec, in the example of a conquered province held by arms. But, alas! when

when they were so ready for war, they little thought, or could be made to understand, what sort of a war it would turn out; and much less would they believe how many other circumstances of persons and things, besides the operation of their arms, would interpose, and become part of the business, before it came to the issue of a settlement.

In like manner, none of the Powers of Europe, and, I believe, very few of the most knowing politicians have considered in a general view, the effect of the present combination of events, or what effect it is likely to have, on the general system of European politics: and yet there is one thing palpably certain; that, on whatever ground the present war between Britain and the House of Bourbon may set out, or in whatever line it takes its course; that, however long, to their mutual ruin, they may continue the contest, by which they hope to decide, to which of them *as allies, fœdere inequali,* the Americans shall belong, the Americans will belong to neither.. The Powers of Europe, who will become parties, before these affairs come to the issue of peace, will concur in no other final settlement, than that these States are an independent sovereign Power, holding a free commerce equally with all.

In order then to shew, how these matters which are like to agitate all the States of Europe, and, if they go to war on this subject, to become the scourge of the present age, how those matters may be settled, without going to war, *and will be finally settled,* whatever are the ruinous, cruel, and destructive operations, and efforts of arms. I, a man long withdrawn from business, and now, at this time, from the world, will endeavour to lay before those whom it may concern, a view of the European and American worlds, comparing their respective systems in the forms under which they exist, and operate to power; and from thence to point out what will be the natural effects of the separation of them, and of the independence of America actuating her system, as it may affect the commercial and political state of Europe; and finally to demonstrate how, if the present crisis be wisely managed, and with a spirit of good-

will

will to Men, it may be wrought into the greateſt bleſſing of peace, liberty, and happineſs, which the world hath ever yet experienced in the courſe of its exiſtence.

In the ſituation in which I find myſelf detached from all connections in the intereſts or politics either of Europe or America; and, as to my locality, in a * meridian between the two worlds, I can look to either as I turn to the eaſt or weſt: freed from thoſe old habits of thinking, or rather of prejudging, which an European is mechanically fettered with, I can, with the ſame philoſophic indifference, with which an aſtronomer examines the comparative matter and magnitude of two diſtant planets, compare theſe two diſtant worlds in their magnitude, ſpirit, and power.

When I ſpeak of greatneſs in the one or other, I mean (as Mr. Bacon, the Lord Verulam expreſſes it) the *amplitude and growth of ſtates*. This ſubject, the comparing the greatneſs of two continents, which never came into compariſon before, is

* At the Azores.

is not more novel in the matter, than I shall be thought to be visionary in the manner and argument; I must therefore march here with formal and measured steps.

Before I enter into this comparison of the amplitude and growth of the states of the old and new world, I shall here premise, what the same noble author suggests, and which, in the course of reasoning, will be explained. "That in the measuring and balancing of greatness, too much is ascribed to largeness of territory on one hand; and on the other, too much to the fruitfulness of soil, or abundance of commodities."

Under this caution premised, I shall state first the *natural greatness* of the new world compared with that of the old.

Greatness without connection of parts is expanse not greatness: natural connection of parts without an actuating intercommunion of those parts, is encumbered bulk, not strength. That greatness of dominions which hath a natural *capability* of systematic connection, by an actuating intercommunion which arises also from nature, can
alone

alone be considered as that *natural greatness* which administers to *amplitude and growth* of states.

Although the three geographical separate parts of the world seem *naturally* to concentre by the Mediterranean sea into a connected communion; and although when and while they were actuated by * an effort of wisdom, as extensive in the branches, as in the communion, at the root, they were combined into a one dominion; yet that being an effort beyond the common holding strength, beyond the ordinary resources of human nature, the scale proved in the end too large for either the spirit or the arm of Man to extend to. It could not but prove to be, in the event, what it was in the moment of its exertion, a predominancy of artificial power against nature, and therefore temporary. The three parts of the old world, Europe, Asia, and Africa, seem to have a natural division in the natural scite and circumstances of their territory. They are also inhabited and possessed by three different and distinct

species

* The policy of the Roman state.

species the of human being. They have, therefore, generally by the effect of principles of nature operating against the vigour of man, fallen, in dominion, into their natural division. North America and South America are, in like manner, at the *fond*, naturally divided into two distinct systems, and will, as naturally, divide into two distinct dominions. On the contrary, large as the scale of North or South America is, neither of these respectively, either in the natural scite and circumstances of territory, nor in the people who possess and cultivate them, are so divided. North America (I speak of the predominating inhabitancy) is possessed by the English nation. South America by the Spanish and Portuguese, which, in this argument, may be called one nation. These natural circumstances in country and people, form each of these divisions of the new world respectively, into a one great communion, the basis of a great and powerful dominion; stretching out its arms and branches over the whole land, as the fibres of the roots interweave into, and through, the various combinations

of

of natural objects, whence they draw their spirit of life.

There is no where in the European part of the old world such a greatness of interwoven and combined interest, communicating through such largeness of territory, as that in North America, possessed and actuated by the English nation. The northern and southern parts of Europe, are possessed by different nations, actuated by different spirits, and conducted under very different systems. Instead of actuating an intercommunion by an attractive, their intercourse is at perpetual variance under a repellant principle; their communion also is obstructed by the difficulties of intercourse both over land, and through the seas; they are moreover cut off, as it were in the middle, by other intervening nations, whose principles and system are alike repellant and obstructive of free communion.

On the contrary, when the scite and circumstances of the large extended territories of North America are examined; one finds every thing united in it which forms greatness

ness of dominions, *amplitude and growth of state.*

The nature of the coast and of the winds upon that coast, is such as renders marine navigation, from one end of its extent to the other, a perpetually moving intercourse of communion: and the nature of the rivers which open (where marine navigation ends) an inland navigation which, with short interruptions, carries on a circulation throughout the whole, renders such inland navigation but a further process of that communion; all which becomes, as it were, a one vital principle of life, extended through a one organized being.

While the country, by the *capability* of this natural communion, becomes thus united at its root; its largeness of territory, expanded through such a variety of climates, produces, upon this communion, every thing that nature requires, that luxury loves to abound in; or that power can use, as an instrument of its activity. All those things which the different nations in Europe (under every difficulty that a defect of natural communion, under every obstruction

struction that an artificial and perverted system threw in their way) barter for in the Old World, are here in the New World possessed, under an uninterrupted natural communion, by an unobstructed navigation, under an universal freedom of commerce, by one nation. The naval stores, the timber, the hemp, the fisheries, the salted provisions of the North; the tobacco, rice, cotton, silk, indigo, finer fruits, and perhaps, in no very distant period, the wines, the resin and tar of the South, form the reciprocation of wants and supplies of each respectively. The bread corn, the flour, the produce of agriculture in every form of farming, and the several encreasing articles of manufactures, which the middle colonies produce, not only fill up the communion, but compleat its system. They unite those parts which were before connected, and organize (as I have said) the several parts into a one whole.

Whether the islands, in those parts called the West Indies, are naturally parts of this North American Communion, is a question, in the detail of it, of curious speculation, but

but of no doubt as to the fact. The European maritime powers, however, if they can adjuſt their reſpective intereſts in thoſe parts; if they will form a balance of power there on thoſe intereſts; if they can ſettle any ſyſtem of reciprocal ſupport of that balance; may certainly, by efforts of force, for ſome years, perhaps for an age longer, preſerve the property and dominion of theſe iſlands. But if their quarrels amongſt each other reſpecting North America, or the European ſhifting of the balance, make them obſtinately deaf to their mutual intereſts in theſe parts, " The " whole of the Spaniſh, Dutch, Daniſh, " French, and Britiſh eſtabliſhments, indiſ- " ſolubly bound in an union and commu- " nion of a one general compoſite intereſt " with North America, and forming the na- " tural connections under which their mu- " tual intereſts ſubſiſt, muſt in the courſe " of events become parts as of the *communion*, " ſo of the great North American *dominion*, " eſtabliſhed on the baſis of that union." Although no external ſymptoms of revolution in South America do at preſent make it any part of the ſubject which I offer to conſideration,

consideration, yet it may not be amiss to inquire into those internal circumstances of its natural and political system, by which its Communion has amplified, and works to independency and the growth of state.

The continent of South America has still more amplitude of basis, in more variety of climates, than North America, and is much farther advanced to a natural independence of Europe, *as to its state of supply*, than the powers of Europe do see, or at least own; or than its own inhabitants, speaking of them generally, are themselves conscious of. This continent, not only from the great extent of latitudes under which it lies, but from the great variety of climates that it experiences under the same latitudes; from the abundance and variety of articles of supply which these different climates produce; from the regular, uniform, and active marine communion, by which a compleat reciprocation of mutual supplies is circulated from North to South, is also formed into one system of communion, the germ of a great independent dominion; that has taken root, is every day ſtriking deeper, and more expanded fibres; and is every day, by the vigour of natural vegetation (if I may ſo expreſs myſelf) putting forth its extended branches, and is growing *occulto velut arbor ævo*, into the greateſt amplitude of communion, and of dominion founded thereon, which this earth hath ever yet ſeen, China perhaps alone excepted. Agriculture in the elevated parts of this country, nearly the ſame as other the perfectly cultivated parts of the world actuate, has taken place, and is in progreſſive motion to the moſt varied and extenſive operations. Theſe parts afford not only abundance for home conſumption, *but a ſurplus for exportation*. The articles of this export are wheat, flour, barley, wine, hemp, tallow, lard, ſugar, cocoa, fruits, ſweatmeats, pickles, naptha, oil, cotton, &c. This progreſs of agriculture hath, in the true courſe of nature, called forth, even from the hands of Indians, manufactures and trade, the roots which ſupply a moſt extenſive circulation of commerce: Cordage, ſailcloth of cotton, woollen and linen cloth, hats, leather, and particularly ſole-leather,

leather, fiance, inftruments of hufbandry, tools of mechanics, and, in fhort, every thing which the advancing cultivation of man's being calls for, from thefe articles.

As the markets, population, and culture of the feveral provinces of the kingdom of Chili (advancing with accelerated, tho' not great, velocity) fhall mutually encreafe each other. The produce of thefe higher latitudes and cooler climates will enter into the great fyftem of intercommunion of fupplies, and will compleat the weftern fide of South America, poffeffed by one nation, into an object of as much greater magnitude, in activity, wealth, and power, than the Englifh nation poffeffes in North America, as it is greater in the variety and extent of its internal communion. Befides which it will have an un- uninterrupted intercourfe of Eaft Indian commerce.

If any accident fhould happen to abate, or give a turn to, the caprices, luxury, and vanity of a rich people, who have nothing to do but to fpend their money, there is not any one article which I can recollect, neceffary to the moft advanced ftate of life, which they

they have not, or may not have, within themſelves. Look back and ſee if this ſtate of the country is not ſo far forth *naturally* independent of Europe, as to all ſupply and ſupport of its exiſtence; I will here add, much more ſo than North America is. The communion in North America has not as yet gone into an *active ſtate* of manufactures, nor will it for many years to come. And yet, on the other hand, although North America is not ſo independent of Europe in the matter of its ſupply and commerce, as South America is, yet being more ſo in the ſpirit of its people, in the œconomy and advance of its political community, it has, with the forcing aid of the government of its metropolis, become the firſt fruit of thoſe who ſlept, and has *only firſt* ſeparated from the old world. South America is not yet in its natural courſe, ripe for falling off; nor is it likely, from the ſlow, official, cautious prudence of its metropolis, to be forced before its time and ſeaſon to a premature revolt, as North America has been. As long as the Spaniſh monarch proceeds in adminiſtring the affairs and the government of

its

its American eſtabliſhments, with the temper, addreſs and wiſdom which it obſerves at preſent, an indolent, luxurious, superſtitious people, not much, (though much more than the public in general ſuſpects) accuſtomed to think of political arrangements, will continue in a certain degree of ſubjection to government, and in a certain degree of acquieſcence to commercial reſtrictive regulations in their European intercourſe, for the ſake of a reciprocity of advantage, enjoyment, and protection, which they derive from it. Not being yet *hardened into a temper for enterprize by force of war*, they will continue to pay their taxes *as a peace-offering*. But the natives encreaſing in numbers, beyond any proportion of the number of Old Spaniards, which the metropolis can ſend either as civil governors and magiſtrates, or as ſoldiers; having the executive power of all the inferior magiſtracies in their own hands, by their own election of the magiſtrates; and having invariably, where their choice operates, a decided rule to chooſe thoſe of their own body; they have, ſo far as that goes, all *the power of*

of internal government in their own hands, in which the majefty of the fovereign power never interferes; and whatever fovereignty the Spanifh monarch holds by the offices of his viceroys, of his judges, of his audiencies, his clergy, or his army, however majeftic they may look, or however it may appear to individuals, and, in particular exertions, carry terror: it *is a mere tenure at good-will.* A great country like this, where the community has fo far advanced in agriculture, manufactures, arts, and commerce, wherein there is fuch *amplitude and growth of ftate,* is every day growing too large for any government in Europe to manage by authority, at the diftance of four or five thoufand miles. And as to the idea of power by force, I will ufe Mr. Bacon, the Lord Verulam's explanation of it; " There be, (faith he) two
" manners of fecuring of large territories;
" the one by the natural arms of every pro-
" vince; and the other by the protecting
" arms of the principal eftates; in which
" latter cafe, commonly the provincials are
" held difarmed. So are there two dangers
" incident unto every eftate, foreign inva-
fion,

"sion, and inward rebellion. Now, such
"is the nature of things, that these two re-
"medies of state do fall respectively into
"these two dangers, *in case of remote pro-
"vinces:* For if such a state rest upon the
"natural arms of the provinces, it is sure to
"be subject to rebellion or revolt; if upon
"protecting arms, it is sure to be weak
"against invasion." And I will venture to
add, weak and *inferior to the internal power*
of the province, which must of course predominate. The Spanish government knows,
that they, as well as the English, found
themselves under the necessity of repealing
an arrangement of revenue which they had
made; because they felt that they *could not
carry it into execution by authority*, and they
so rightly understood their strength, as to
know that it was *not safe to urge it by force.*
It is also very well known, that the disputes
between the Spanish and Portuguese courts,
about the boundaries of the Brazils and the
Spanish provinces, arose from their not being
able jointly to carry into effect a pacification
on the case, because there are Powers in
those countries, who would not be bound
by the decisions of a government, whose

D   laws

laws are of no authority with them, when oppofed to their fyftem. The powers I mean, are the governing authority of the miffions at Paraguay. This is exactly and precifely the ftate of the cafe between the metropolitan government of Spain and its provincial eftablifhments in South America. I could, by a detailed defcription of the nature of the country; of the application of the labour of the inhabitants to its *capabilities*; of the ftate of the community as it lies in nature, and as it is actuated; all compared with the conftitution and adminiftration of the government which is eftablifhed there; with the fpirit of the people, both Old Spaniards, Creoles, and Indians, fhow that South America is growing too much for Spain to manage; that it is *in power*, to be independant, and will be fo *in act*, whenever, and as foon as any occafion fhall call forth that power. Whenever fuch revolt takes place, it will not be after the manner or in the form of that of North America. North America building on the foundation of its dominion as it lies in nature, has become a Democratick or Ariftocratick Republick. The falling off of South America will be conducted,

in

in *its natural* progrefs, by the fpirit of fome injured enterprizing Genius, taking the lead of a fenfe of alienation and of a difpofition of revolt, to the eftablifhment of a great Monarchy. But all this is befide the fcope of this memorial, and would become of itfelf a long memoire. I fhall proceed therefore to confider only thofe operations which are in event, the *amplitude and growth of ftate* in North America, fo far as the ftates and whole political fyftem of Europe may be affected by it, or concerned in it. I have ftated this *natural* greatnefs, as it is founded in an union of a communion. The civilizing activity of the human race, is what forms the growth of ftate.

To balance the *comparative progrefs of the growth of this ftate* with thofe of Europe, fo as to obtain any juft idea of a fubject, even yet fo little underftood, it will be neceffary to take a view of this *civilizing activity*, in the fources whence it derived upon the old world; in the line its progrefs took, and in the defective eftablifhments to which, even in this enlightened age, it is but yet arrived: and, to compare that with the progrefs and extended fcope of a very different civilizing activity,

activity, operating with rapid and accelerated motion in the new world.

When the spirit of civilization began first in Europe, to emerge from that chaos of barbarism and ignorance, which the Northern invaders, like an overwhelming deluge, had spread over the face of it; the clergy sent from Rome, as missionaries amongst savages, were the blind leaders to light; and the selfish feudal Lords, the patrons of liberal emancipation. Under such auspices, what light, what liberty, what civilization! The instruction of the first, derived through a perverted channel of learning, from a corrupted source of knowledge, which being directed not to inform, but to subdue the mind, was more pernicious than the darkness of ignorance, than the aberrations of barbarism *. The kind patronage of the latter, was the benevolence of a grazier, who feeds and fattens his cattle, in order to profit the more of their fleeces, hides, and carcase. The instruc-

* Si ad fructum nostrum referemus, non ad illius commoda, quem diligimus. Prata & Arva & pecudum greges diliguntur isto modo, quod fructus ex iis capiunter. Cicero de Nat. de. Lib. 1. p. 44.

tion of thofe teachers was the dictates of authority impofed upon mere cataceumens, *homines dedititiis.* Their learning was didactive, not as that of the new philofophy and new world is, inductive: their knowledge was a mere paffive impreffion of maxims and principles, which, though neither explained nor reafoned upon, being reiterated, became opinions, formed into fyftem, eftablifhed in inveterate habit. The people held, did not poffefs, their knowledge, as they did their lands, by a *fervile tenure,* which did not permit them to ufe or improve it as their own. They were fettered by authority, led aftray by example, and under a felfifh felf-obftructing fyftem, wafted every power of activity in unavailing labour: fuch was the *fource* of civilization in Europe.

In order to view the two lines of its *progrefs* in Europe and in America, it may be proper to mark and draw, as far as may be done, a third line, to which both have reference in the comparifon, the right line. In the natural progrefs of this civilizing activity, the firft movement is, the application of labour to the culture of the earth, fo as to to raise by a cultivated, production of its fruits, that supply of food which is necessary to the human being in society. That labour which builds habitations, provides rayment, and makes tools and instruments, which the human hand wants the aid of, is concomitant with this. The market traffic, by which the reciprocation of wants and surplusses of various articles in various hands, may be wrought into a communion of general supply, succeeds to these. Individuals being thus assured of their supply, by an assurance of the exchange of the surplus, which each is able to create in his own peculiar line of labour, will soon improve the craft of their hand, and refine the ingenuity of their designs. Hence, by a further advanced step, arise, what are properly called, artificers and manufacturers. In this state of the progress of the community, a general surplus, not only beyond what individuals, but beyond what the wants of the community require, is created: and this general surplus, as it may be exchanged for foreign articles of comfort and enjoyment, which the locality and climate of that particular

ticular community does not produce, extends and opens a courfe to commercial activity, which is the next ftage in this progrefs.

With a reference to this line, view now the civilizing activity of the new and of the old world, each in its fource and progrefs.

By the violence of the military fpirit, under which Europe was a fecond time peopled, the inhabitants were divided into two claffes, thofe of warriours and flaves, and the individuals (each man under their own clafs) were as of different degrees fo, of different denominations.

The culture of the earth was conducted by this latter clafs, wretches annexed to, but not owners of the foil; degraded animals that were, as the cattle of the field, property, not proprietors. They had no intereft in their own perfons, none in their own labour, none in the produce, either of the earth or of their labour. If they had been infpired (for they were not taught) with knowledge, they could have no one motive to make one effort of improvement. Moreover, even thofe who were in fome
degree

degree emancipated, that is, thofe to whom their kind Lords had lett leafes of their ownfelves, were fo depreffed by various tolls, taillages, and taxes; by being liable to military impreffes; and to the civil drudgery, which took them from their own proper work, and employed them in that of thefe Lords and fovereigns; which wore and tore their cattle and carriages and implements of hufbandry; were, I fay, fo depreffed, that the very beft fpirit of them could aim at nothing in the interval but bare fuftenance and reft: if yet this unfubdued fpirit, working, under fuch burthens, with unabated perfeverance or ingenuity, ever did by the remnant of their exertions raife a furplus in grain or cattle: This miferable race of men were precluded all vent and market except fuch, wherein their Lords were to abforb the chief profits, even of fuch furplus alfo. The confequence therefore was, that they never did *by intention* raife fuch furplus; accidents of extraordinary feafons, or fome of the hidden fecrets of vegetation, would now and then produce fuch a furplus; but more frequent accidents

accidents of the same kind did occasion a deficiency and dearth. The police of these great Lords never suffered the homely wisdom of this little adage to enter into their reasoning, " *That he who would have a com-* " *petency, should provide enough and a little* " *more.*"

The progress therefore of improvement in agriculture was arrested, and became for many hundred years stationary. Although in some countries of Europe it may seem at present to be progressive; yet is the progression so little and so Low that it can give no momentum, for ages to come, to amplitude and growth of state, England perhaps excepted. But the farmer in England also is, equally as absurdly as cruelly, oppressed and kept down.

The work of man employed on wood, iron, stone, or leather, were held as parts of the base and servile offices of society; and fit only for the bondsmen and slaves, to whom such were committed. These artificers or handicraftsmen therefore were mere machines in the hands of the most arrogant as well as the most ignorant of masters.

E They

They could not venture to make experiments, or alter the adopted and accustomed mode of work: they would have no merit, nor receive either reward or private profit from their success, and they risqued every thing in the failure; so these branches of mechanicks and art went on for ages in the old beaten track of the same unimproved clumsiness.

When upon the breaking up of the Hanseatic League and other shiftings of commerce, the Sovereigns, who had long with envy seen, but never understood, the profit and power which arose from manufactures brought forward into trade, began to encourage their own subjects, and to invite foreign ones to establish manufactures within their respective states; and, with what they thought profound policy, to conduct the commerce of such; civilization then took in this line of improvement a momentary start of progression. But the wretched condition under which this profound and jealous policy held the persons of these manufactures, the many depressing, obstructing, impracticable regulations, by which it restrained

their

their labour, foon gave a retrograde motion to thefe efforts. The fame policy, however affecting to give encouragement to thefe manufactures, which it had forced into operation before and fafter than the country was ripe for them, not out of its own purfe, but from the fweat and fuftenance of the landworker, gave the manufacturers a falfe help, by fetting various affizes on the produce of the land, and by various market regulations, which ftill further oppreffed agriculture. But all this was falfe and hollow, for, added to all the depreffions of mind and obftructions of body which thefe poor manufacturers fuffered, there was yet an adventitious heart-breaking cruelty, to which even merit was peculiarly expofed. If ever ingenuity of mind, or an excelling habit in the hand of any of thefe artificers or manufacturers, invented fomething new or operated to fome improvement in the old line of work; The fame jealous tyrannous police, inftead of rewarding them, or fuffering them to feek their own reward, condered them, not as meritorious authors of good and benefit to the community, but as profitable

profitable inftruments to feed their private avarice; and inftantly guarded them as ftate prifoners. The poor ingenious Artift found himfelf reduced to a ftate worfe than flavery, for the ingratitude of fuch governments embittered even oppreffion. The confequence was, that all further improvements, here alfo, were arrefted in their courfe. As though all this was not yet fufficient to keep down all fpirit in the arts, and all progrefs of improvement, this fyftem of police made regulations to be obferved and taxes to be paid on every movement of the manufactures after they were made; on their coming from under the hand of the workman; on the carriage; on the expofing to fale; on the fale; and on the return, whether in goods or money. This police, inftead of fuffering the furplus profit to circulate freely through the community, where it would become a growing fource of accretion and fructuation to that community, was intirely directed to abforb the whole, beyond the labourer's hard fuftenance, into the treafury of the ftate. The idea which they entertained of the utmoft perfection of the commercial

mercial fyftem, was, that the fubject fhould fell but not buy; that the merchants might export the articles of their work, but muft import money: and that the ftate muft have the greateft fhare of it. The whole fcope and effort of all their commercial legiflation, was pointed to arrive as near as poffible to this imagined perfection. Under thefe ideas, and under the authority of maxims, grown inveterate, they took up the idea of commercial police, and adding the myftery of politicks to the myftery of trade, began to legiflate for commerce. Hence arofe the attempts to fet up exclufive property in certain materials of manufacture and trade, which they called ftaple commodities: hence incommunicative monopolies in every fhape that the ingenuity of ignorance could invent to mock the induftry of its country with: hence exclufive privileges of trade to certain perfons in certain articles and in certain places: hence exclufive fifheries: hence all that nonfenfe, both in theory and practice, in which commercial politicians have taken fo much pains to deceive themfelves, about a chimera, called

the

the balance of trade; hence all the cunning follies, which rendered their markets almoſt impracticable to each other; and hence, to double and redouble the miſchief, the whole train of retaliations. Hence reſtraints on exportation, prohibitions againſt importation, alien duties, high impoſts, and a thouſand other embarraſſing follies, of which there is no end or uſe. Having thus, in their ſtruggles for profit, deranged all the order of prices; having ſet out with a falſe balance of reckoning; having by reciprocal retaliation, rendered the free courſe and fair competition of commerce, well nigh impracticable amongſt themſelves, they were forced to look out for ſettlements amidſt ſome yet uncivilized or uncommercial people, where they might exerciſe this unequal ſpirit of exorbitant gain: hence alſo treaties of commerce, on unequal conditions of traffic, with thoſe of their neighbours, whom they could keep down depreſſed by aſcendant power: and hence, finally, the grand and favourite meaſure of eſtabliſhing colonies in diſtant uncultivated regions, which, as out-farms of peculiar production, might be worked

for

for the sole exclusive benefit of the metropolis: hence also that wildest of all the wild visions of avarice, inspiring ambition, the attempt to render the common ocean an object of enclosed, defined, exclusive property, and to claim a possession in, and dominion over it. Thus, through want of reference to the light of nature, from not seeing and treating things as what they were; from a total inversion of the natural order of progress in the human community; the culture of the natural powers of the land; the improvement of the natural powers of man, to the end of advancing the community; the order and establishments, or rather the liberty, whereby a civilizing activity might operate to the amplitude and growth of states, were all depressed or arrested in their progress. The very spirit of improvement was buried under oppression, and all the light of genius extinguished. Those who presumed to reason, being such as were at the head of the received knowledge, such as had the lead of the received opinions, and conducted the policy of the established systems, considered the subject as a matter fully explored, and as founded in the furest and most decided wisdom. Their ascendant authority, whether they spoke as politicians, or philosophers believing what they taught, did equally lay a dead hand on all examination, did extinguish all attempts of alteration to improvement. Moulded by habits, almost mechanical, to think and act in the line of these established systems, efforts of reasoning did but the more entangle them, in delusive means taken, and ineffectual ends proposed. They did but strive against themselves, to save the credit of ignorance, and to satisfy themselves in the poverty of their knowledge. Instead of following nature to those truths on which profitable labour, progressive civilization, population, opulence, strength, and the real interest of their country might be established, their best wit was employed only to vary old irreversible mazims, and to give new forms to old established systems, or at best by new regulations, to relieve the interests of the subject, who could no longer go on, or endure, under the old ones. But as the credit and authority of the system is yet to be kept up, the ingenuity and wit of

those

thofe, who pay their court to Power, is still employed in finding out new and striking reasons for old maxims, or inventing fictions and cases for reconciling old establishments, to new modes of acting in them, which fact, truth, and irresistible neceffity, have introduced in practice. If any genius ever dare to break this spiritual subordination, and to pursue, either in speculation or practice, any new course to truth or action; all those who lead the opinions of this settled world, must either affect to contemn him as a silly visionary foolish, inexperienced adventurer, or crush him as a presumptuous, turbulent, dangerous disturber of the State.

This is the state of the spirit of civilizing activity, as it hath long dragged on a feverish being in Europe, in the old world. Some time or other (and perhaps soon) events may arise, which shall induce the Governors and leaders of that corner of the world to revise, to consider, and perhaps to reform the hard conditions of its imprisonment, and to give it liberty, free as its

G   native

native essence. In the mean while we will turn our eyes westward,

In this new world we see all the inhabitants not only free, but allowing an universal naturalization to all who wish to be so; and an uncontrouled liberty of using any mode of life they choose, or any means of getting a livelihood that their talents lead them to. Free of all restraints, which take the property of themselves out of their own hands, their souls are their own, and their reason; they are their own masters, and they act; their labour is employed on their own property, and what they produce is their own. In a country like this, where every man has the full and free exertion of his powers, where every man may acquire any share of the good things thereof, or of interest and power which his spirit can work him up to; there, an unabated application of the powers of individuals, and a perpetual struggle of their spirits, sharpens their wits, and gives constant training to the mind. The acquirement of information in things and business, which becomes necessary

cessary to this mode of life, gives the mind, thus sharpened, and thus exercised, a turn of inquiry and investigation which forms a *character peculiar to these people*, which is not to be met with, nor ever did exist in any other to the same degree, unless in some of the ancient republics, where the people were under the same predicament. This turn of character, which, in the ordinary occurrences of life, is called *inquisitiveness*, and which, when exerted about trifles, goes even to a degree of ridicule in many instances; is yet, in matters of business and commerce, a most useful and efficient talent. Whoever knows these people, and has viewed them in this light, will consider them as *animated in this new world* (if I may so express myself) *with the spirit of the new philosophy*. Their system of life is a course of experiments; and, standing on that high ground of improvement, up to which the most enlightened parts of Europe have advanced, like eaglets they commence the first efforts of their pinions from a towering advantage.

Nothing in the old world is lefs regarded than a poor man's wifdom; and yet a rich man's wifdom is generally nought but the impreffion of what others teach him: On the other hand, the poor man's wifdom is not learning, but knowledge of his own acquiring and picking up, and founded upon fact and nature by fimple experience. In America, the wifdom and not the man is attended to; and *America is peculiarly a poor man's country.* Every thing in this wildernefs of woods being totally different from an old world, almoft worn out; and every perfon here far removed from the habits, example, and perverfion, or obftruction, of thofe who affume the power of directing them: the fettler's reafon, not from what they they hear, but from what they fee and feel. They move not but as Nature calls forth their activity, nor fix a ftep but where ufe marks the ground, and take the direction of their courfes by that line only, where Truth and Nature lead hand in hand. They find themfelves at liberty to follow what mode they like; they feel that they can venture

to

to try experiments, and that the advantages of their discoveries are their own. They, therefore, try what the soil claims, what the climate permits, and what both will produce and sustain to the greatest advantage. Advancing in this line of labour *by such a spirit of induction,* they have brought forward into culture an abundant produce, more than any other nation of the old world ever did or could. They raise not only abundance and luxurious plenty to their internal supply, but the islands of the West Indies have derived great part of their supply from the superabundance: even Europe itself hath, in many articles of its supply, profitted of the produce of this new world. It has had its fish from their seas; its wheat and flour from one part; its rice from another; its tobacco and indigo from another; its timber and naval stores from another: olives, oranges, wines, and various other articles of the more luxurious produce, having by experience been found to thrive, *are in experimental culture.*

If you view this civilizing spririt in its first simple movements, you will see it as
in

in its first infancy, so attaching itself to the bosom of the common mother Earth, as the infant hangs upon the breast of its natural mother. The inhabitants, where nothing particular diverts their course, *are all landworkers.* Here one sees them labouring after the plough, or with the spade and hough, as though they had not an idea beyond the ground they dwell upon; yet is their mind, all the while, enlarging all its powers, and their spirit rises as their improvements advance.* He, who has observed this progress of this new-world, will know that this is true, and will have seen many a real philosopher, a politician, or a warriour, emerge out of this wilderness, as the seed rises out of the ground, where it hath lain buried for its season.

As in its agriculture, so in those mechanick handicrafts, which are necessary to, and concomitant with that, the new world hath been led to many improvements of implements, tools, and machines: a deficiency of many of these, an inaptitude in

* I hope no one will so misunderstand this, as to take it for a fancy-drawing of what may be; it is a lineal and exact portrait of what actually exists. Editor.

in many of those, which they are able to get, has put these settlers, many times to their shifts; and these shifts are experiments. The particular use which calls for some succedaneum, or for some further alteration, leading experience by the hand to improvement, hath opened many a new invention. While this spirit of thus analysing the mechanic powers, with the sole and simple view to effect (instead of plodding on with a mere mechanical habit, of old implements, tools, and machines, generally clumsey, and oftentimes inapplicable) hath established *a kind of instauration of science* in that branch; more new tools, implements, and machines; or rather more new forms of such have been thus invented in this new world, than were ever yet invented in the old, within the like extent of country in the like space of time. Many instances of this fact might be here specified in the higher, as well as in the common, diurnal mechanics.

This new world hath not yet turned its labour into the *active* channel of arts and manufactures; because by employing that
labour

labour in its own natural way, it can produce thofe things which purchafe fuch articles of arts and manufactures, cheaper than a country not yet ripe for thofe employments, could make them. But although it doth not manufacture *for fale,* the fettlers find intervals and *fragments of time,* which they can fpare from agriculture, and which they cannot otherwife employ, in which they make moft of the articles of perfonal wear and houfhold ufe, *for home confumption.* When the field of agriculture fhall be filled with hufbandmen, and the claffes of handicrafts fully flocked; as there are here no laws that frame conditions on which a man is to become entitled to exercife this or that trade, or by which he is excluded from exercifing the one or the other, in this or that place; as there are here no laws that prefcribe the manner in which, and the prices at which, he is to work, or that lock him up in that trade which it has been his misfortune to have attached himfelf to; although while he is ftarving in that, he could, in fome other line of bufinefs which his circumftances

stances point out, and his talents lead him to be useful to the public, and maintain himself; as there are none of those oppressing, obstructing, dead-doing laws here: the moment that the progress of civilization, carried thus on in its natural course, is ripe for it; the branch of manufactures will take its shoot, and will grow and increase with an astonishing exuberancy.

Although the civilizing activity of America does not, by artificial and false helps, contrary to the natural course of things, inconsistent with, and checking the first applications of, its natural labour, and before the community is ripe for such endeavour, attempt to force the establishment of manufactures: yet following, as Use and Experience lead, the natural progress of improvement, it is every year producing a surplus profit; which surplus, as it enters again into the circulation of productive employment, creates an accumulating accelerated progressive series of surpluses. *With these accumulated surpluses* of the produce of the earth and seas, *and not with manufactures,* the Americans carry on their *commercial*

mercial exertions. Their fish, wheat, flour, rice, tobacco, indigo, live stock, barrel pork and beef (some of these articles being peculiar to the country and staple commodities) form the exports of their commerce. This has given them a direct trade to Europe; and, with some additional articles, a circuitous trade to Africa and the West Indies.

The same ingenuity of mechanic handicraft, which arises concomitant with agriculture, doth here also rise concomitant with commerce, and is exerted in SHIP-BUILDING: it is carried on, not only to serve all the purposes of their own carriage, and that of the West Indies in part, but to an extent of sale, so as to supply great part of the shipping of Britain; and further, if it continues to advance with the same progress, it will supply great part of the trade of Europe also with shipping, at cheaper rates than they can any where, or by any means, supply themselves.

Thus their commerce, although subsisting (while they were subordinate provinces) under various restrictions, by its advancing pro-

progress in *ship-building*, hath been striking deep root, and is now shot forth an *active commerce*, growing into *amplitude of state* and great power.

Stating the ground on which an objection is made to this description of the improving commerce of America, will open to view another extraordinary source of *amplitude and growth of state*. It will be said, that the fact of the balance of trade, being at all times, and in every channel, finally against America, so as to draw all the gold and silver it can collect from it, is but a damning circumstance of its progressive advance in commerce and opulence. In the first place, is it not a fact, that America (even while partitioned out into depressed and restrained provinces) has carried on all its advanced culture in a progress to great opulence; and has it not been constantly extending the channels of its trade, and encreasing its shipping? There is not a more fallacious and misguiding maxim (although it has been adopted in practice, and even by commercial nations) than that of judging of the general balance of profit in commerce, by the movements of that one article of it, *the precious metals*. This *metallic money*, as the traffic of the world is generally conducted, is an article as neceſſary to go to market for, as any other article whatſoever. In the general circulation of trade, it will always, as any other article of commerce doth, go to that country which pays the moſt for it. Now that country which, on any ſudden or great emergency, wants money, and knows not how to circulate any other money than the metallic, muſt pay the moſt for it. Conſidered under this idea, the influx of this article into a country, inſtead of being the ſymptom, or conſequence, of the balance of trade being in favour of that country; or the efflux being the mark of the like balance, being againſt it, may be a fact in proof of the contrary. The balance of trade, reckoned by the import or export of gold and ſilver, may, in many caſes, be ſaid to be againſt England, and in favour of thoſe countries to which its money goes. If this import or export was really the effect of a final ſettled account, inſtead of being,

as

as is generally the cafe, only the carrying and deducting of this article to or from fome open current account, having further reference; yet would it not be a mark of the balance of trade. England, from the nature of its government and the extenfivenefs of its commerce, has eftablifhed a credit, on which, on any emergency, it can give circulation to paper money almoft to any amount. If it could not, it muft, at any rate, purchafe gold and filver, and there would be a great influx of the precious metals. Will any one here fay, that this ftate of its circumftances is a mark of the balance of trade being in its favour: but, on the contrary, having credit from a progreflive balance of profit, it can, even in fuch an emergency, fpare its gold and filver, and even make a profit of it as an article of commerce exported. Here we fee the balance of profit creating a credit, which circulates as money, even while its gold and filver are exported. If any particular event, as for inftance, the late one of the recoinage of the gold in England, which called in the old coin at a price better than

that

that at which it was circulating abroad, should raise the price of this article in England, it will, for the same reason as it went out, be again imported into England; not coming as the balance of their accounts, but as the article of trade, of which the best profit could at that moment be made. The fact was, that at that period, quantities of English gold coin, to a great amount, were actually imported into England in bulk; and yet this was no mark of any sudden change of a balance of trade in favour of that country.

The balance of trade, reckoned by this fallacious rule, has been always said to be against North America also: but the fact is, that the government of that country, profiting of a *credit arising from the progressive improvements, and advancing commerce of it* (which all the world sees, or it would be no credit) hath, by a refined policy established a circulation of paper-money to an amount that is astonishing; that from the immense quantity it should depreciate, is nothing to this argument; *for it it has had its effect.* The * Americans, therefore, as well as England, can spare their gold and silver, can do without it. The efflux, therefore, of the precious metals, is no proof of its being a balance against them. On the contrary, they being able to go on without gold and silver, but wanting other articles, without which they could not go on, neither in the progression of their improvements, in the advance of their commerce, nor in the conduct of their war matters; the metallic money is in part hoarded, and in part goes out, and those articles of more use to them are imported. Does it not then turn out to be a fact, that this objection, which is always given as an † instance of weakness in America, under which she must sink, turns out, in the true state of it, an instance of the *most extensive amplitude and growth*

---

* My information says, that there is now locked up in America more than *Three Millions*, English money, in gold and silver species, which when their Paper is annihilated will come forth. Editor.

† Would it not be well for England, if while she triumphs over this mote in her sister's eye, she would attend to the beam in her own, and prepare for the consequences of her own Paper Money! Editor.

growth of state, which would not have been considered, or even seen, had the objection not been made.

I will here, therefore, from this comparison of the spirit of civilizing activity in the old and in the new world, as one sees it in its application to agriculture, handicrafts, and mechanics, and finally in an active commerce, spatiating on an amplitude of base, the natural communion of a great country, and rising in a natural progression, venture to assert, that in this point, NORTH AMERICA HAS ADVANCED, AND IS EVERY DAY ADVANCING, TO GROWTH OF STATE, WITH A STEADY AND CONTINUALLY ACCELERATING MOTION, OF WHICH THERE HAS NEVER YET BEEN ANY EXAMPLE IN EUROPE.

But farther; when one looks to the progressive POPULATION which this fostering happiness doth, of course, produce, one cannot but see, in North America, that God's first blessing, " *Be fruitful and multiply; replenish the earth and subdue it,*" hath operated in full manifestation of his will. In Europe, on the contrary, where a wretched, selfish, self-obstructing policy, hath

hath rendered barren, not only fruitful countries, but even the womb itſelf; one may ſay, in melancholly truth, that the firſt curſe, "I will greatly multiply thy ſorrow in procreation; in ſorrow ſhalt thou bring forth children," ſeems to have been executed in judgment. That wretched ſtate of the country and people, which hath rendered fruitfulneſs a matter of ſorrow, and children a burthen, hath arreſted the progreſs of population. The apprehenſions of having a family to ſupport when the poor parents know not where or how to provide a home and ſuſtenance; the dread of bringing into the world (objects ſo dear to all parents) who are to be born in a ſtate not much better than ſlavery, hath palſied the very idea of marriage, the fruits of which are to be brought forth in ſorrow. * In North America children are a bleſſing, are riches and ſtrength to the parents; and happy *is every man that hath his quiver full of them.* As the nature

---

* Magnum quidam eſt incitamentum, tolere liberos in ſpem alimentorum, majus tamen in ſpem libertatis, in ſpem ſecuritatis.

Plin. Paneg. 1. § 27.

and caufes of this amazing population hath been fo fully difcuffed, and with decided demonftration, explained in *" Obfervations concerning the increafe of mankind, the peopling of countries, &c."* I fhall refer thofe who think it neceffary to purfue this point of the comparifon further, to that little treatife; and fhall proceed here to confirm it by examples of the actual encreafe ftated in authentic facts.

The province of *Maffachufett's Bay* had inhabitants in the year

   1722-----94,000
   1742----164,000
*   1751----164,484
   1761----216,000
   1765----255,500
   1771----292,000
   1773----300,000

In the colony of CONNECTICUT the inhabitants, at the beginning of laft war, and of the prefent, ftood

   1756-----129,994
   1774-----257,356

Obferve here, that the numbers, by which

           thefe

---

* N. B. A great depopulation, by the fmall-pox and war, in that period.

thefe people have thus encreafed, are not aided by any accretion of ftrangers; but, on the contrary, they appear lefs than they would actually be, if all thofe people whom the colony loft in the courfe of laft war, and all thofe who, in very great numbers, emigrated to the weftward fince the war, could have been added; as it is, they have encreafed nearly the double in eighteen years. As it may be a matter of curiofity, and not irrelevant to the argument, I will here infert a particular inftance of fecundity in a family in Connecticut. Mary Loomis (or Loomax) born at Windfor in Connecticut - - - - 1680
Married John Buel of Lebanon in do. 1696
Died at Litchfield in do. - - 1768

Defcendants living at her death:

Child.	Gr. Child.	G. Gr. Child.	Fourth Gen.
10	75	232	19
Died bef. her			
3	26	42	3
13	101	274	22

Tot. defcendants { Alive at her death 336
{ Died before her 74

Tot. encreafe born - - 410

The Province NEW YORK.
1756------96,776
1771------168,007
1774------182,251.

The Dominions of VIRGINIA.
1756------173,316
1764------200,000
1774------300,000

The Province of SOUTH CAROLINA.
1750------64,000
1770--- *115,000

The Colony of RHODE ISLAND.
1730------15,302
1748-9----28,439.

As there never was a regulated general militia in PENNSYLVANIA, which could enable thofe, whofe bufinefs it was, to get accounts of the increafe of population in that province, founded on authentic lifts, it hath been varioufly eftimated on fpeculation. Although there was a continued import.

* This is fuppofed to be below the actual number, the great increafe of population being, in the back countries, not then included in the regulations of the policy. Editor.

Import for many years of Irish and Foreign emigrants into Philadelphia (of which I have the numbers) yet, informed as I am, that many of these passed through the province, and settled either directly, or as soon as their indented service expired, in other provinces, I think the progress of population may be reckoned here also by the ordinary course of procreation, as in other provinces and colonies; and by collating different estimates, I think I may venture to say, that its population, when I was in the country, advanced in a ratio between that of Massachusett's-bay and Virginia. The city of PHILADELPHIA, indeed, from circumstances of trade, advanced with a more rapid motion, of which fact the following is a statement in proof.

PHILADELPHIA had in the year houses
Inhabitants on estimate ⎰ 1749 2076
from 16,000 to 18,000 ⎱ 1753 2300
31,318 to 35,000 ⎰ 1760 2969
⎱ 1769 4474

To speak of the population of the country in general; there were at the beginning of the war, 1754 and 5, various calculations and estimates

mates made of the numbers of the people on the continent. Thofe who were fanguine, and thought they could correct the materials from which the eftimate was to be made, fancied they were juftified in making the amount of the numbers of the people *one million and a half.* Thofe who did not admit fo much fpeculation into the calculation, but adhered clofer to the facts of the lifts as they were made out, could not ftate the amount at more than one million two hundred and fifty thoufand.

The eftimate of the numbers of the people, faid to have been taken by Congrefs in September, 1774, makes them 3,026,678; but when I fee how that account, from which the eftimate is made, differs, in many particular articles, from what I have ventured to ftate as authentic returns, I am convinced that there muft have been great fcope of fpeculation taken and allowed in that eftimate. I have feen another eftimate which makes the number, at a later period, after two or three years of war, 2,810,000. In what I am going to advance, I am myfelf rather

reafoning

reasoning upon estimate than authentic fact, for I have not seen the returns of *all* the provinces; yet from what I have now seen, compared with what I have known formerly, I do verily believe, and therefore venture to say, that 2,141,307 would turn out the number nearest to the real amount in the year 1774. But what an amazing progress of population is it, which, in eighteen or nineteen years, has added near a million of people to a million two hundred and fifty thousand, although a war was maintained in that country for seven years of that period.

In this view, one sees again the amplitude of the community unfolding its progressive increase and growth of State, beyond any example that any of the Powers of Europe can bring into comparison in the account.

But more; these numbers are not a mere multitude of dwellers, *fruges consumere nati*. The frame and model of these communities, which hath, from the first establishment of them, always taken place, (Pennsylvania excepted) is such as hath
enrolled

enrolled every common subject, by the poll, to be a soldier; and, by rotation of duty, has *trained,* to a certain degree, a quarter part, or about 535,326 *of these people to the actual use of arms,* so that the country has this number not separate from the civil community, and formed into a distinct body of regular soldiers, but remaining united to the internal power of the community, as it were, *the national picquet guard,* always prepared for defence. I am aware, that even these numbers, being the numbers of a mere militia, will appear contemptible to the regular Captains and Generals of Europe; yet, experience in fact hath always evinced that, for that very reason, that they are not a separate body, but members of the body of the community, they became *a real and effective national defence,* have toes that are roots, and arms which will bring forth the fruits of external protection, with internal security and peace. This establishment is an organized part of the body, and can be maintained at all times, and even in time of service, at little more expence than

the

the ordinary vital circulation requires. The real greatneſs and ſtrength of the State ariſes from and conſiſts in this * " that every common ſubject, by the poll, is fit to make a ſoldier, and not certain conditions and degrees of men only." I cannot cloſe this part of my reaſoning better than in the ſentiment in which the ſame great Stateſman and Philoſopher gives his opinion on the matter, " The true greatneſs of the State conſiſteth eſſentially in population of breed of men, and where there is valour in the individuals, and a military diſpoſition in the frame of the community; where all, and not particular conditions and degrees only, make profeſſion of arms, and bear them in their country's defence."

Great as this amplitude of the community may be at its baſe; far advanced as it may be in the progreſs of its civilizing activity; eſtabliſhed in intereſt and power as it may be by an active commerce; and ſecurely fortified as it may ſeem in the union of its military ſpirit; yet all this, without the ſoul of Government, would prove but

K   a

* Ld. Verulam.

a phantom. So far as the vitality of Government can animate the organized being, and so far as the spirit of Government can actuate the will of the whole, so far, and no farther, can the amplitude and growth of the State extend.

If the dominions of an Empire be extended, while, by reason of a narrowness or weakness in the vital spring of Government, the spirit of Government cannot so extend, as to give vital union to its distant parts, or, by an union of will, to actuate the *consensus obedientium* in those remote parts, the extension of the dominions works not to amplitude and growth, but to the dissolution of State. Such Government will call those remote parts, external provinces; and because it hath not the virtue or the vigour to so extend the spirit of Government to them, as that, while they obey the will, they feel themselves vitally united to it, it will assume the tone of Force. But as the natural internal force will not act against itself, that is not the force which Government in such case can use; Government, brought into such an

unhappy

unhappy cafe, muft attempt therefore to act by external, unnatural force fent from without. But, alas! any force that (even with violent temporary exertions) it can fend to thefe extremities (without draining itfelf at heart) will bear no comparifon with the natural internal force of thofe provinces, and can have no effect but that of alienation and diffolution. When fuch a cafe exifts, the dominions of an Empire, which were not too great for a right fpirit of Government, but which, actuated by that fpirit, was in a continual progreffion to amplitude and growth of State, are foon found too great for the falfe and unnatural fpirit of Force. Let us here view this world (by the fatality here defcribed) now feparated and fallen off from that vital union by which it was once an organized member of the Englifh Empire: let us view it *as it now is*, AN INDEPENDENT STATE *that hath taken its equal ftation amidft the nations of the earth*; as an Empire, the fpirit of whofe government extends from the centre to its extreme parts, exactly in proportion as the will of thofe parts doth reciprocally unite in that center. Here we shall find (as hath always been found) "That universal participation of council creates reciprocation of universal obedience. The seat of government will be well informed of the state and condition of the remote and extreme parts; and the remote and extreme parts, by participation in the legislature, will from self-consciousness, be informed and satisfied in the reasons and necessity of the measures of government. These parts will consider themselves as acting in every grant that is made, and in every tax which is imposed. This consideration alone will give efficacy to government, and will create that *consensus obedientium*, on which only the permanent power of the imperium of a state can be founded: this will give extension and stability of empire as far as it can extend its dominions."

This might have been, indeed, the spirit of the British Empire, America being a part of it: *This is the spirit* of the government of the new Empire of America, Great Britain being no part of it. It is a Vitality, liable, indeed, to many disorders,

many

many dangerous diseases; but it is young and strong, and will struggle, by the vigour of internal healing principles of life, against those evils, and surmount them; like the infant Hercules, it will strangle these serpents in its cradle. Its strength will grow with its years, and it will establish its constitution, and perfect adultness in growth of state.

To this greatness of empire it will certainly arise. That it is removed three thousand miles distant from its enemy; that it lies on another side of the globe where it has no enemy; that it is earth-born, and like a giant ready to run its course, are not alone the grounds and reasons on which a speculatist may pronounce this. The fostering care with which the rival Powers of Europe will nurse it, ensures its establishment beyond all doubt or danger.

Where a state is founded on such amplitude of base as the union of territory in this new world forms; whose communion is actuated by such a spirit of civilization, where all is enterprize and experiment; where

where Agriculture, led by this spirit, hath made discoveries in so many new and peculiar articles of culture, and hath carried the ordinary produce of bread-corn to a degree that has wrought it to a staple export, for the supply of the old world; whose fisheries are mines producing more solid riches, to those who work them, than all the silver of Potosi; where experimental application of the understanding, as well as labour to the several branches of the mechanics, hath invented so many new and ingenious improvements; where the Arts and Sciences, Legislation and Politics, are soaring with a strong and extended pinion, to such heights of philosophic induction; where, under this blessedness, Population has multiplied like the seeds of the harvest; where the strength of these numbers, taking a military form, "*shall lift up itself as a young lion;*" where Trade, of a most extensive orbit, circulated in its own shipping, hath wrought up this effort of the Community to an *active Commerce;* where all these powers unite and take the form of establishment of Empire; I may suppose that I cannot err, nor give offence to the

greatest

greatest Power in Europe, when, upon a comparison of the state of mankind, and of the states of those Powers in Europe, with that of America, I venture to suggest to their contemplation, that America is growing too large for any government in Europe to govern as subordinate; that the Government of North America is too firmly fixed in the hands of its own community, to be either directed by other hands, or taken out of the hands in which it is: and that the power in men and arms (be they contemned or contemptible, as the wisdom of Europe may suppose) is too much to be forced at the distance of three thousand miles.

If I were to address myself to a philosopher, upon a supposed adventitious state of the planetary system, and ask him, whether, if an accretion of matter should enlarge any satellite till it grew into magnitude, which balanced with its primary; whether that globe, so encreased, could any longer be held by any of the powers of nature in the orbit of a secondary planet; or whether any *external force* could hold it

thus

thus reftrained; he will anfwer me directly, No. If I afk the father of a family, whether, after his fon is grown up to man's eftate, to full ftrength of body equal to the parent, to full power of mind and vigour of reafon; whether he can be held in the fame fubordinate pupillage, and will fuffer himfelf to be treated, under correction, as aforetime in his childhood? The father will be forry to be afked the queftion, and be willing to evade it; but he muft anfwer, No. Yet, if I afk an European politician, who learns by hearfay, and thinks by habit, and who fuppofes of courfe that things muft go on, as they have always gone on; whether, if North America, grown up, by a diftinct and independent intereft in their œconomy and commerce, to a magnitude in nature, policy, and power, will remain dependent upon, and be governed by, any of the metropolitan ftates on the other fide of the globe; he will confidently anfwer, Yes. He will have ready a thoufand reafons why it muft be fo, although fact rifes in his face to the very contrary. There have

been

been, and there are, periods in the History of Man, when, instead of *the politician* being employed to find out reasons to explain facts, he and all about him shall be *busied to invent, or make, facts, that shall suit predetermined reasonings*. Truth, however, will prevail, and things will always finally prove themselves to be what they are.

What has been here said is not meant to establish proof of the *Fact, which is in event*; but so to explain it, as that the consequences of it may be fairly and clearly seen. As to the existence of the facts, or the effect of them in operation, it is of no import. THE PRESENT COMBINATION OF EVENTS, whether attended to or not, whether *wrought by wisdom* into the system of Europe or not, *will, forcing its way* by the vigour of natural causes, *be found there* in all its ascendant operations. These will have their effects, and Europe in the internal order and œconomy of its communities, in the courses of its commerce, will be affected by it. The statesman cannot prevent its existence, nor resist its operation. He may embroil

his

his own affairs; but it will become his beſt wiſdom and his duty to his ſovereign and the people, that his meaſures coincide and co-operate with it.

The firſt of the conſequences is, the Effect which this Empire, in a new and ſeparate world, *become a great naval Power,* will have on the commerce, and perhaps by changes introduced in that, on the political ſyſtem of the old world.

Whoever has read and underſtands any thing of the ſtate of the Hanſeatick League in Europe, and conſiders it's progreſs, firſt by it's poſſeſſing all the commanding articles of the commerce of the then world, and the commercial command of all the great rivers through which that commerce muſt circulate; next it's being the carrier of the trade of Europe; and finally it's forming, on this aſcendant intereſt, by the means of it's ſhipping and ſeamen, *an active naval Power,* that in all caſes could attract the intereſt of, in many caſes reſiſt, and even command the landed Powers; whoever, viewing this, conſiders that this League was made up of a number of towns, separate from, and unconnected with each other, and included within the dominions of other Powers and States, of a number of individual towns, who had *no natural communion*, and only a forced and artificial union amongst each other; whoever, duly marking this at the basis, follows the progress of the power, not only commercial but naval and political, which this League, under all these natural disadvantages, established throughout all Europe, will be at no loss to see on how much more solid basis the power of North-America stands founded, how much faster and with more rapid increase (unobstructed with those difficulties which the League met with) it must grow up, and to what an extent and ascendancy of interest, carrying on the greatest part of the commerce, and commanding the greatest part of the shipping of the world, this great commercial, naval, American Power must soon arrive at. If this League, without having the natural foundation of a political body, a landed root, could grow, by an active commerce and the effect of navigation, to such

such power as we know it did possess, and acted with; if this League, of parts separated by Nature, and only joined by the artificial cement of force, could become a great political body, existing, as it were vitally, by a set of regulations of *internal* police, and acting *externally* with an interest and power that took a lead, and even an ascendancy in wars and treaties, what must the States of North-America, removed at a distance of almost half the globe, from all the obstructions of rival Powers, having at it's root a landed dominion, *peculiarly adapted to the communion of commerce and union of power*, and already grown up in an almost universal active commerce, rise up to in their progress? As this Hanseatick League grew up to power, Denmark, Sweden, Poland, and even France, sought it's alliance (under the common veil of pride) by offers of becoming it's Protectors. England also, growing fast into a commercial Power, had commercial arrangements, by treaty, with it. Just so now will the Sovereigns of Europe, just so now have the great

Bourbon

Bourbon Compact, the greatest Power in Europe, courted the friendship of America. Standing on such a basis, and growing up under such auspices, one may pronounce of America as was said of Rome, *Civitas, incredible est memoratu, adeptâ libertate quantum brevi creverit.*

I mark here *what may be in event*, from a view and consideration of *what has been in fact*, merely to obviate a suspicion of my reasoning being theory and vision.

In the course of this American war, all the Powers of Europe (at least the maritime Powers) will, one after another, as some of the first leading Powers have already done, apply to the States of America for a share in their trade, and for a settlement of the terms on which they may carry it on with them. America will then become the ARBITRESS of the commercial, and perhaps (as the Seven United Belgic Provinces were in the year 1647) the *Mediatrix of peace*, and of the political business of the world.

If North America follows the principles on which Nature hath established her; and
if

if the European alliances which she has already made do not involve her in, and seduce her to, a series of conduct destructive of that system, which those principles lead to; she must observe, that as Nature hath separated her from Europe, and hath established her *alone on a great continent, far removed from the old world, and all its embroiled* interests and wrangling politics, without an enemy or a rival, or the entanglement of alliances* "I. That it is contrary to the nature of her existence, and of consequence to her interest, that she should have any connections of politics with Europe, other than merely commercial; and, even on that ground, to observe invariably, the caution of not being involved in either the quarrels, or the wars of the Europeans in Europe. II. That the real state of America is, that of being the common source of supply *to Europe in general;* that her true *interest* is, therefore, that of being a FREE PORT to all Europe at large; and that all Europe at large should be THE COMMON MARKET for American

* Common Sense.

merican exports. The true intereft, therefore, of America is, not to form any partial connexions with any part to the exclufion of the reft."

If England had attended to her own intereft, as connected with that of America, fhe would have known, that "it is the commerce, and not the conqueft of America, by which fhe could be benefitted;" and if fhe would, even yet, with temper, liften to her true intereft, fhe would ftill find, " that that commerce would, in a great meafure, continue with the fame benefit, were the two countries as independent of each other as France and Spain, becaufe, in many articles, neither of them can go to a better market."

What is here faid, is fpoken of them, as influenced under their prefent habits and cuftoms of life :---Alienation may change all this.

Be thefe leffer private interefts difpofed of, as the fate of kingdoms determines: The views of this memoir are directed only to the general confequences of the general combination of events.

The

The firſt, which in all human probability will, ſooner or later, become the great leading principle between the old and new world, is, that North America will become a FREE PORT to all the nations of the world indiſcriminately; and will expect, inſiſt on, and demand, in fair reciprocity, a FREE MARKET in all thoſe nations with whom ſhe trades. This will, (if ſhe forgets not, nor forſakes her real nature) be the baſis of all her commercial treaties.

If ſhe adheres to this principle, ſhe muſt be, in the courſe of time, the chief carrier of the commerce of the whole world; becauſe, unleſs the ſeveral powers of Europe become to each other, likewiſe, FREE PORTS and FREE MARKETS, America alone will come to and act there, with an aſcendant intereſt that muſt command every advantage to be derived from them.

The commerce of North America being no longer the property of one country only, where the articles of its ſupply were either locked up, or came thence to market through a monopoly; theſe articles will

come

come freely, and be found now, in all the markets of Europe at large; not only moderated by, but moderating the prices of the like articles of Europe. The furrs and peltry will meet thofe of the north-eaftern parts of Europe; and neither the one nor the other can any longer be eftimated by the advantages to be taken of an exclufive vent. Advantages of this kind, on the article of *iron*, and on *naval ftores*, have frequently been aimed at by Sweden; and the monopoly in them was more than once ufed as an inftrument of hoftility againft England. This occafioned the meafure which the Parliament of that country took of granting bounties on thefe articles, the growth and produce of America, which meafure gave fource to the export of the fame articles from North America: thefe, when they come freely to the European markets, co-operating with the effect which thofe of Ruffia have there, will break that monopoly: for Ruffia alfo, by the conqueft of Livonia, and the advancement of her civilization, has become a fource of fupply in thefe fame articles to a great extent. All Europe,

Europe, by the *intervention of this American commerce* in her markets, will find the good effects of *a fair competition, both in abundance of supply, and in moderation of price.* Nay, even England, who hath lost the monopoly, will be no great loser on this score: she will find this natural competition as advantageous to her, as the monopoly which, in bounties, and other costs of protection, she paid so dear for.

Ship-building, and the science, as well as art of navigation, having made such progress in America, so that they are able to build and to navigate cheaper than any country in Europe, even cheaper than Holland with all her œconomy can, there will arise in Europe a competition, at least in this branch of commerce. In this branch the Dutch will find powerful rivalship from that maritime people, the Americans. The Dutch will also find, in the markets of Europe, a competition in the branch of the *Fisheries*.

The *rice* and the *bread corn* which the Americans have been able to export, to an amount that supplied, in the European market,

ket, the defect arising from England's withholding her exports, will, when that export shall again take place, keep down depressed the agriculture of Portugal and Spain, and, in some measure, of France also, if the policy of those countries does not change the regulations, and order of their internal œconomy.

The peculiar articles of supply to be had as yet from America only, and which the markets of Europe so much seek after and demand, will not only give to the Americans the command of the market in those articles, but enable them, by annexing assortments of other articles of commerce, to produce these latter articles also, with preference and advantage in those markets.

The *refuse fish*, *the flour*, *the maize*, the *barrelled meat*, the *live-stock*, and *various lesser articles of subsistence*, and the *lumber*, all carried in American shipping to the West-India Islands, directly from North America: the African slaves carried, by a circuitous trade, in American shipping also, to the West-India markets: the taking from thence the melosses; and the aiding those islands with American shipping, in the carriage also of their produce, must ever command and have the *afcendancy in the commerce* of that part of the world; if this afcendancy even ftops here.

But to clofe the confideration of the effects which the *commercial activity* of this New Empire will have, one may fum up all in this, that the cheap manner in which the Americans can, at prefent, produce their articles of fupply; the low rates at which they can carry them to the European markets, felling alfo their fhipping there; the fmall profits at which their merchants are content to trade, muft lower the price of the like articles in the European market; muft oblige the European merchant alfo to be content with lefs profit; muft occafion fome reform of the home œconomy of Europe in raifing, and of the order of Police in bringing to the market, the native articles of fupply of that Continent. But further; thefe people by their principle of being a *free port* in America, and having a *free market* in Europe; by their policy of holding themfelves, "as they are remote from all the wrangling politics, fo neutral in all the wars of Europe:"

by

by their spirit of enterprize in all the quarters of the globe, will oblige the nations of Europe to call forth within themselves such a spirit, as must change entirely its commercial system also.

But will a people whose Empire stands singly predominant in a great Continent; and who, before they lived under their own Government, had pushed their spirit of adventure in search of a North-West passage to Asia, which, as being their own discovery, they meant to have claimed as their own peculiar right: will such a people suffer in their borders the establishment of such a monopoly as the European Hudson's Bay Company? Will that enterprizing spirit, which has forced a most extensive commerce in the two Bays of Honduras and Campeachy, and on the Spanish main, and who have gone to Falkland's Islands in search only of whales, be stopped at Cape Horn, or not pass the Cape of Good Hope? It will not be long after their establishment as an Empire, before they will be found trading in the South-Sea and in China. The Dutch will hear of them in Spice Islands,

Iflands, to which the Dutch can have no claim; and which thofe enterprizing people will conteft, on the very ground, and by the very arguments which the Dutch themfelves ufed to conteft the fame liberty againft Portugal.

By the conftant intercommunion that there will be between Europe and America; by the conftant correfpondence and growing acquaintance that there will be towards the latter, it will be as well known, in general, as Europe: by the continual paffage to and from that Continent; by attention to the nature of the winds, which, however variable, have their general courfes; by repeated obfervations on the currents in the Atlantic, which (befide the general current of the Gulf ftream and its lee-currents) fet according to the prevailing winds, in various courfes between the fhoaler and broken ground; the paffage will be better underftood, and become every day fhorter; America will feem every day to approach nearer and nearer to Europe. When the alarm which the idea of going to a *ftrange* and a *diftant* country gives to the homely notions of an

European

European manufacturer or peasant, or even to those of a country gentleman, shall be thus worn out, a thousand repeated repulsive feelings, respecting their present home; a thousand attractive motives, respecting the settlement which they will look to in America, will raise a spirit of adventure, and become the irresistible cause of an almost *general Emigration to that New World*. Nothing but some future, wise, and benevolent policy in Europe, or some spirit of the evil one, which may mix in the policy of America, can prevent it.

The Great Creator hath stationed a Cherubim, with a flaming sword, that turns every way, and meets man at every avenue through which he would pass in quitting life itself. Unless the great Potentates of Europe can station some such universal, and equally efficient, power of restraint to prevent man's quitting this Old World, multitudes of their people will emigrate to the New One. Many of the most useful enterprizing Spirits, and much of the active property will go there also. Exchange hath taught the statesman of the world long ago,

that

that they cannot confine money: and the ſtate of the Empire of theſe European ſtates muſt fall back to an old feudal community, in which its own people are locked up, and from which all others are excluded, or *commerce will open the door to Emigration.* The Sovereigns of Europe, who are cognizant of thoſe movements, and who know how to eſtimate their effects, muſt feel what an adventitious weight hence, alſo, will be added to the encreaſing ſcale.

Such, upon a patient inveſtigation through paſt experience doth the ſtate and circumſtances of things, in Europe and in America reſpectively, appear to the Writer of this paper: ſuch, upon a comparative view of the two worlds, in thoſe points which lead to amplitude and growth of ſtate, doth the combination of events, in which they are mixed, appear. The Memorialiſt attempts not to reaſon upon the matter. He aims only, and that with all humility, to point out to the contemplation of thoſe who muſt act upon it, and who ſhould therefore reaſon, the natural, or, at leaſt, probable tendency of effects flowing

from

from it: and how these relations of things ---*Legesque et fœdera rerum,* are forming what he conceives will be the New System. He is neither so unpractised in the world, no so absurd, as to attempt to establish these practical truths by argument. He knows the influence that settled principles and decided maxims have on the public as well as private opinion, that men measure every degree of proof, and even demonstration itself, by them. The sublime politician, who spatiates in the regions of predetermined systems, which no experience can ever enlighten, will not stoop to reason. The man of the world, narrowed by a selfish experience, which is worse than ignorance, will neither reason nor feel. Besides, if individuals had direct and practical conviction of the existence of the facts herein stated, and did actually feel the truth of the effects; yet it requires something more materially operative to move collective bodies of men. It is but slowly that nations relinquish any system which hath derived authority from time and habit; and where that habit passes for experience, and that authority for truth.

When contrary effects, constantly and uniformly opposing themselves to the activity of error, shall make men hesitate, and raise some suspicions *that all is not right in the old system:* when Experience, observing (as it were) two ships sailing on the great ocean, shall see that while the sails of the *one*, instead of being so set as to draw together, and to give the vessel its due course, do counteract each other, and obstruct its course; that it is repeatedly taken a-back, and with all its bustle and activity makes but little way; the *other*, setting all its sails *as* the *nature* of the elements *requires*, and so as all to draw together, doth, in a one quiet unshifting trim, and in a one uniform steady course, make great way; so as to sail down the other out of sight: when Experience, having observed this, shall apply it to what he may observe in the different effects of the different systems of the Old and New World; Reason will be heard, Truth will have its force, and Nature act with all its powers. Until some great event shall produce this frame and temper of mind in the European world,

world, all reasoning will become the mere theory of a visionair; all argument the downright impertinence of an obtruding missionair.

Those Sovereigns of Europe who have been led by the office-systems and wordly wisdom of their Ministers; who seeing things in those lights, have despised the unfashioned aukward youth of America; and have neglected to form connections, or at least to interweave their interests with those of these rising states: when they shall find the system of this New Empire not only obstructing, but superseding the old system of Europe, and crossing upon the effects of all their settled maxims and accustomed measures, they will call upon these their Ministers and wise men, " *Come curse me this people, for they are too mighty for me.*" Their statesmen will be dumb, but the spirit of truth will answer, " *How shall I curse whom God hath not cursed? Or how shall I defy, whom the Lord hath not defied? From the top of the rock I see them, from the hills I behold them. Lo! the people shall* DWELL ALONE, *and shall* NOT BE RECKONED AMONGST THE NATIONS." America is separated from Europe; she will dwell alone: She will have no connection with the politics of Europe; and she will not be reckoned amongst the Nations.

On the contrary, those Sovereigns of Europe who shall call upon their Ministers to state to them things *as they do really exist in Nature,* and treating those *things as being what they are,* shall require of these Ministers, that they take their system from Nature, instead of labouring in vain, to the misery of mankind the mean while, to force Nature to their predetermined courses and system: And who shall be in such circumstances and situation, as to be able to form, if not the earliest, yet the most sure and natural connection with North America, as being, what she is, AN INDEPENDENT STATE, THE MARKET OF AND A FREE PORT TO EUROPE; AS THAT BEING WHICH MUST HAVE A FREE MARKET IN EUROPE, will (coinciding with the movements, and partaking of the effects of the new system) become

the

the principal leading Power in Europe, in regulating the courses of the rest, and in settling the common center of all.

England is the State that is in those circumstances and in that situation; the similar modes of living and thinking, the same manners and same fashions, the same language and old habits of national love, impressed in the heart and not yet effaced, the very indentings of the fracture whereat North-America stands broken off from her, all conspire naturally to *a rejuncture by alliance.* If, in the forming that juncture, England, no longer assuming to be what she no longer is, will treat America, and all other Beings, as what *they really are*, she might still have the ascendancy in trade and navigation, might still have a more solid and less invidious power than that

Magni Nominis umbra

with which she braves the whole world; she might yet have an active leading interest amongst the Powers of Europe. But she will not. As though the hand of judgment was upon her, England *will not see the things which make for her peace.*

France,

France, on the contrary, already (and other States will follow this example) *acknowledging thofe States to be what they are,* has formed alliances with them on terms of perfect equality and reciprocity. And behold the afcendant to which fhe directly rofe from that politic humiliation.

There never was a wifer or firmer ftep taken by any eftablifhed Power, than that which the New States in America took for their *firft footing* in this alliance; there never was more addrefs, art, or policy fhewn by any State, than France has given proof of in the fame; when both agreed and became allied on terms which exclude no other Power from enjoying the fame benefits, by a like treaty.

Can it be fuppofed that other States, conceiving that the exclufive trade of England towards America is laid open, will not defire, and will not have, their fhare of it, and of the benefits to be derived from it? They certainly will. Here then come forward *the Beginnings of changes* in the European fyftem.

There are too courfes in which this
general

general intercommunion of commerce, betwixt Europe and North-America, may come into operation: the one will lye in special and particular treaties of commerce, with specific regulations and tariffs, made separately, from time to time, with each separate State: the other may come into operation by ALL THE MARITIME STATES OF EUROPE, either previous to, or in consequence of such separate treaties; either previous to their engaging in a general war, or upon the general settlement of a peace, MEETING IN SOME CONGRESS to regulate, amongst themselves, as well as with North-America, the FREE PORT, on one hand, and the FREE MARKET on the other; as also, general regulations of commerce and navigation, such as must suit *this free-trader, now common to them all, indifferently, and without preference.* Such regulations, in the first place, must exclude all monopoly of this source of supply and course of trade; and so far make an essential change in the commercial system: such regulations, not having reference only to America, but reciprocal references between

tween all the contracting parties, trading now under different circumstances, and standing towards each other in different predicaments, must necessarily change the whole of that system in Europe.

The American will come to market in his own shipping and will claim *the ocean as common;* will claim a *navigation restrained by no laws but the law of nations,* reformed as the rising crisis requires; will claim *a free market,* not only for the goods he brings, whencesoever he brings them, but also for the ships in which he brings them; the sale of his shipping will make part of his commerce. America being a free port to all Europe, the American will bring to Europe *not only his own peculiar staple produce,* but every species of his produce which the market of Europe can take off: he will expect to be free to offer to sale in the European market, every species of wrought materials, which he can make to answer in that market: and farther, as his commerce subsists, and is carried on by a circuitous interchange with other countries and regions, whence he brings articles,

cles, not simply for his own consumption, but as exchangeable articles, with which to trade in foreign markets; he will claim, as one of the conditions of the *free market*, that these foreign articles, as well as his own produce, shall be considered as free for him to import in his own shipping, to such market. Those States who refuse this at first, seeing others acquiesce in it, and seeing also how they profit by having articles of supply and trade brought so much cheaper to them, will be obliged, in their own defence, and to maintain their balance in the commercial world, to accede to the same liberty. Hence again, even if the American should not, by these means, become the ascendant interest in the carrying-trade, and in shipping and seamen, a most essential change must arise in the European system.

Again; the American raises his produce cheaper, and navigates cheaper, than any other can: his staple commodities are articles which he *alone* can supply; these will come to the market assorted with others, which he thus can *most conveniently* supply; and, unless the same liberty and freedom

O of

of trade, which he enjoys, be reciprocally given and taken, by the European Powers, amongſt each other, he will come to the European market on terms which no other can.

Nor is it in the articles which the American brings to ſale, but in his manner of trading for thoſe articles which he purchaſes, that the community in Europe will be affected, benefitted, and improved. There will be found not only a fair competition in the ſales, but the *peculiar activity* of the American will raiſe, of courſe and as neceſſary, a ſpirit and activity amongſt thoſe who come to the ſame market. That peculiar turn of character in the American, before deſcribed, that inquiſitiveneſs, which in buſineſs animates a ſpirit of inveſtigation to every extent, and in the moſt minute detail, wherever information is to be had, excites and enables them to conduct their dealings in trade in a different and more advantageous manner than is uſually practiſed by the European merchant. They acquire a knowledge not only of the markets of Europe, that is, of the wants and

and fupplies, how they correfpond, and of their relative values; but they never reft till they are poffeffed of, in the moft minute degree, a knowledge of every article of produce and manufacture which comes to thofe markets; until they know the eftablifhments, the operations, and the prices of labour, and the profits made on each, as well, or even better than merchants of the country themfelves. This ftate of information, joined to their commercial activity, leads them to the immediate fources of all the fupplies they want to purchafe, without going through the channel of a foreign merchant or factor.

A little time before the breaking out of the troubles between England and America, feveral of the American merchants, efpecially thofe of Pennfylvania, fending fome of their own houfe to England (as I am informed) became their own factors, went immediately to the manufacturers in Birmingham, Wolverhampton, and Sheffield; to the woollen manufacturers in Yorkfhire and Lancafhire; to thofe of Liverpool; and to thofe in the Weft; and opened an

O 2 immediate

immediate traffick with them at the firſt hand. This ſame ſpirit of inveſtigation, and this ſame commercial activity will in the ſame manner actuate their dealings in every other country of Europe where they have a free market.

The effect ariſing from this may appear, at firſt view to be diſadvantageous to thoſe countries, and may indeed affect the courſes of the European Merchant individually, but it will become a general bleſſing to the community of every country at large, by being the means of raiſing a more general competition and of diffuſing a more equal or proportional ſhare of profit between all ranks and orders of the induſtrious. While trade is ſolely in the hands of the Merchant, He, not from the nature of the man, but from the nature of trade itſelf, bears hard on the purchaſer by his high rate of profit, and oppreſſes the manufacturer by the bare living ſhare of profit he allows him: the Merchant grows rich and magnificent, makes a great buſtle and a great figure: the eye of the world, attracted by the glare of theſe mercantile in-
ſtances

stances of the advancing opulence in the country, has never accustomed itself to inquire, whether part of this princely magnificence is not derived from the depression of industry, occasioning, at the same time, a certain defalcation from the quantity of goods which would otherwise be produced? It can never be well with any country when the Merchants are Princes, or where the Prince is the Merchant. The more that the Merchant can make by high profits, the less in quantity (on every consideration) will he carry to market. It will be his interest to keep the market scantily stocked; it will become his interest, by the collateral occasion which this will give him, to represent the demand of the market as decreased, for thus he will keep down the manufacturer's profit. Whereas, on the contrary, in the moment that commerce becomes free and open; and, by the intermixture of this American spirit of trade, runs, with fair competition, in a broader channel: The merchant must make his way by being content with small profits, and by doing a deal of business on

those

those small profits. The consumer and the manufacturer will come into more immediate contact, and be known to each other. The one will save the unreasonable advances which he used to pay, and the other will obtain a more equal share of the profits which arise on his labour. More work will be done; the profits of industry more equally distributed; the circulation of the vital nutritious juices will be diffused through the lesser vessels, and give universal life and health, and more perfect exuberance of growth to the whole community.

If these facts be true, and this representation of effects be according to Nature; and if these operations take this course; it will be needless to point out to the shrewd speculations of the merchants, what their conduct must necessarily be; but it will behove the Statesmen in the several Governments of Europe to be aware, that, while this change is in operation, they do not suffer the merchant to persuade them, that the general commerce is languishing and in decay, merely because there is not the same parade of wealth, in such dazzling instances, inftances, in the partial accumulated opulence of particulars. Let them look firft to the market of fupply in fubfiftence, and inquire, whether there is not plenty there ? Next to the rude produce, which is the bafis of manufactures, and inquire, whether, while more and more induftry is daily called forth, it is not employed and more adequately paid by a free and extended vent? And whether, while the number and ingenuity of manufacturers increafes and advances, they do not all live more comfortably, fo as to be able to maintain, and confequently, in fact, to have, increafing families; whether population does not progreffively encreafe, as it meets the fources of induftry in employment and pay. Let them, for the future, guard againft the narrowed intereft and exclufive temper of trade; while they encourage, *by an attractive principle of general communion*, the genuine fpirit and life of commerce.

The Political Founders of the old fyftem in the old world, were totally ignorant of this principle of commerce: they feem not to have underftood how this fruit-bearing

tree

Tree was to be planted, or how to be cultivated. Inſtead of preparing, they wiſhed to impoveriſh the ſoil from whence it ſhould have drawn its nutrition; it was wiſdom with them to render their neighbours and cuſtomers poor. They cramped and mangled the very roots by the various ways in which population was obſtructed. Their impatient avarice ſapped the very bole of its vital fluid, ſo as to drain off that circulation, which ſhould give nutrition and encreaſe to it; by a wretched ſyſtem of taxation, they effectually prevented the ſtock of labour and profit from accumulating. They cut off the bearing branches (the huſbandmen and munufacturers) by dragging thoſe uſeful members to the barren labours of their ſtanding armies. And what little fruit, after all, the poor languid ſtarving Tree could produce, they gathered into monopolizing ſtores, leſt others ſhould ſhare the profit of it. But if the Stateſmen of the preſent more enlightened age will follow where experience, grounded in the actual ſtate of things, leads to truth and right, they will throw the

activity

activity of mankind into its proper courfe of productive labour. When man hath the liberty of exerting his active powers of induftry or ingenuity, as he can make them the moft productive, and finds a free market for what he produces, and his fhare of profit in proportion to his efficiency in creating it, then is the ground duly prepared for the encreafing population, opulence, and ftrength of the community; then will the Sovereigns of this old world find their foundeft intereft, and moft efficient power, arifing into amplitude and growth of ftate, through means of their People's happinefs.

If the Sovereigns of Europe fhould now at length find in the example of England, that the fyftem of eftablifhing colonies in diftant regions and various climates, in order to create a monopoly of the peculiar product of the labour of the people whom they fend thither, *is at an end*; and would turn the fame attention, with the fame zeal, to *colonizing at home*; that is, fhould, like the Police of China, give fource and exertion to their own internal powers

powers of production, should cultivate their waste lands, and improve their agriculture, and in its due turn, give every encouragement to manufacture; if they would abolish all those useless bonds of slavery, which operate in corporations and corporation-laws; which fix down the activity of the human being, as it were a plant, to a local vegetable life, where its real powers are fettered and locked up, which repell all equality and competition, which obstruct or pervert the very spirit of communion, and render those, who should live under it, aliens to each other: As all those wretched remnants of barbarism shall be removed, the productive powers of the community will create those surpluses which will *become the source,* and in the due course of nature, *open* in their turn *the channels of commerce.*

If the European Statesmen, from experience of what has past, and been the effect of the system of Europe; from intuitive experience of the progressive State of America; should see the self-obstruction which arises from attempts to force an *exclusive clufive commerce*; fhould fee, in the examples of Spain and England, the difappointed ends of attempts to eftablifh a *monopoly of navigation by the force of laws,* inftead of creating or maintaining it by the fpirit of an active commerce; fhould fee, that all the meafures of *prohibitions,* by which the feveral States of Europe labour to reprefs the reft, do but deprefs themfelves; They may at length come to a temper in thinking, at leaft, if they cannot yet bring themfelves fo to act, that to give freedom, fcope, and activity to commerce, is the true fyftem for every country, which in its nature and operations is actually commercial.

All this, I know, will be called fpeculation; and it is indeed, at prefent, but mere theory; yet having, by a feries of experience, in repeated inftances, and in fome of great import, feen, that *propofitions which have been contemned and rejected in one country,* have, in their due feafon, become *operative wifdom in another,* I will (hoping that I do not prefume too much) proceed in this fpeculation.

I will

I will suppose, that the Statesmen of the old world, checked at least in their career of war; entertaining some doubts, or hesitation at least, on the principles and maxims of their old system; perceiving that the œconomical activity in Europe is on the turn to take a new course; feeling, in fact, the force and expanding operations of an active commerce; finding themselves under the necessity of making some reform at least, *begin themselves to speculate,* how, amidst a number of Powers of trade, shifting their scale, an even balance may be formed, and secured in establishment; how, amidst a number of fluctuating interests, *buoyant on the turn of this great tide in the affairs of man,* an equal level may be obtained and maintained. If this should lead them to review their old system, and they should perceive how it is of itself prepared for change, perhaps they may find that Commerce, which might have risen by a competition in an active industry, a retentive frugality, and exertions of ingenuity, hath long been an exclusive scrambling rivalship;
that

that * Commerce, inftead of being (as in it's true nature it is) an equal, equable, univerfal operation of communion, which concenters the enjoyments of all regions and climates, and confociates men of all nations, in a one mutual communion of all the bleffings of Providence: when actuated as it hath been, by a repellant felfish principle, hath operated in Europe under the old fyftem, as the golden apple of Difcord, and been to the feveral neighbour nations an occafion of jealoufies of each others powers of enjoyment; alternate depreffions of each others interefts; and a never-ceafing fource of wars for many of the latter ages of the world: perhaps they may alfo then fee that treaties of peace by which thefe have been terminated, are but truces; and that guarantees are but fo many entangling preparations for future wars.

While they cannot but fee things to have been fo, on one hand, they will, I
should

* Quid quod omnibus interfe populis commercium dedit? Ingens Naturæ beneficium, fi illud in injuriam fuam non vertat hominum furor. Sencœ Nat. Queft. Lib. 5 **and** 18.

should however hope, have satisfaction in perceiving, that the manners of mankind, softened and smoothed by degrees, have at length become more humanized; their society and police more civilized; that the world at large hath been rising nearer and nearer, every day, to a meridian which hath enlarged its views, which hath enlightened, and infused a more generous and liberal spirit into it: that although many of the old, oppressive, depressing forms and institutions of Government, as they respect the cultivators of the earth, the manufacturer, the internal market, the merchant and external commerce, have not yet been actually abolished; yet that practice, in the administration of those governments, hath by various accommodations, various facilities, abrogated their worst and most mischievous operations; that the activity of man finds every day more and more, a freer course; that it finds itself encouraged, where it is in a situation so to do, to engage in the culture (if I may so express myself) of the fruitfulness of the seas; that artificers and manufacturers begin to feel motives

which

which not only prompt their induſtry, but encourage their ingenuity; that there are a thouſands ways and channels (which though Pride will not open, Prudence will connive at) through which the intercourſe of markets finds every year a more free and unreſtrained vent; and that the active attraction and free ſpirit of commerce is, like the ſpirit of life, diffuſing itſelf through the whole maſs of Europe. They will find that, in fact, there is an end to all their *monopolizing ſyſtems*; that there is an abſolute impracticability, and total inefficiency in every line and effort of their *repulſive meaſures*. Experience of paſt effects will, in the courſe of this review, mark to them, that any one of thoſe Powers of Europe, who would aim to deal with the reſt of mankind with an unequal balance; who would endeavour to pile up the flow of their commerce in a channel above the level of the circumfluent commerce; will only find in the end, that they have raiſed amongſt their neighbour nations, a ſpirit of jealouſy, a revulſion, and a temper of univerſal rivalſhip, that ſhall conſpire to wreſt

that

that falſe balance out of their hands, and to depreſs them down again, to a level with the reſt of the world. No other effect ever did or could derive from the European ſyſtem of commercial policy; theſe are the univerſal laws of nature, analogous in the moral, to thoſe which operate in the natural world. The cities of Italy, thoſe of the Low Countries, the States of Portugal, Holland, England, have all in their ſeaſon, and for their period, as commercial powers, ariſen above the common level of the reſt of the world; but over-preſſing with a weight which was felt as unequal, by thoſe placed below them; they have each, in its turn, found, even in the moment of their higheſt elevations a general riſing all around them, and themſelves ſinking to the common level.

If the Stateſmen of Europe ſhould, at length, begin to liſten to theſe experiences, and to reaſon on theſe principles, they, reaſoning, not like philoſophers on abſtract theory, but like politicians on the actual ſtate of things, and wrought thus to a temper of treating, and acting towards things

things *as they really are*; they must see how much it is the interest of All, to liberate each other from the *Restraints*, *Prohibitions* and *Exclusions*, by which they have reciprocally aimed to repress, and keep back that industrious activity, or at least the effect of it, which should otherwise have given source, in each respectively, to the common benefit and interest of All: They will see * " that the most advantageous " way which a landed nation" [prepared at the foundation as in this paper described] " can take, to encourage and multiply " Artificers, Manufacturers, and Merchants " of their own, is to grant the most perfect " freedom to the Artificers, Manufacturers, " and Merchants of every other Nation:" That the *Repulsive System*, and *Exclusive Navigation*, on the contrary, lowers the value of their own internal surpluses, by raising the prices of all things which must be bought with them: And gives also to the Artificers, Manufacturers, and Merchants,

Q *a mo-*

---

* Dr. Adam Smith.

a monopoly againſt their own land-workers: Seing this, they will encourage Population, firſt internally, by preparing the ground for the roots, which is the natural and moſt efficacious means, as hath been ſeen in America; next by an univerſal Naturalization and Liberty of Conſcience. Should the Sovereigns of Europe at length ſee this truth manifeſted by experience, which the politicks of Stateſmen, and the myſteries of Tradeſmen, have ſo long hid from their eyes; that *a general and univerſal freedom of Commerce*, under the preſent conſpiring ſtate of the men and things of the commercial world, can operate only to promote in the people of each Nation, the neceſſity of an active induſtry, œconomy, ſobriety, experimental ingenuity, and a temper of equal juſtice, coinciding with the general communion of Commerce; and that theſe virtues while they render each particular national community productive, populous, opulent and ſtrong, do unite the intereſt of the Sovereign and the happineſs of the People, in the power of the State: Elevated as their ſituation is, and above all local, partial

tial views, they muſt ſee, that, if Nature has ſo formed Man, if policy has ſo framed Society, that each labouring in his deſtined and defined line of labour, produces a ſurplus of ſupply, it is the law of Nature and of Nations, it is of perfect juſtice as well as policy, that men and nations ſhould be free, reciprocally to interchange, and reſpectively as their wants mark the courſe, theſe ſurpluſes: that this *Communion of Nations* with each other, by which they aid and profit each themſelves, each other and all, is a right which may be enjoyed and exerciſed in its true and genuine ſpirit, and to its utmoſt extent, except in time of war, but even to great degree in time of war, without interfering in the political and civil power of the world; and that (if ſo) it ought to be thus enjoyed and exerciſed to the benefit and intereſt of each, and to the common good of all.

To thoſe who *ſee things as they are,* and *reaſon upon them as being what they are,* the ſpirit of thoſe *excluſive laws of navigation* which obſtruct an equal ſyſtem of univerſal communion in commerce, will appear as the

the spirit of piracy; will appear in the extreme execution of them at the breaking out of hostilities, and oftentimes even in declared war, the same in the thing and fact as the robberies of those States which the Powers of Europe have decidedly called Piratical: they will see that the COMMON OCEAN, incapable of being defined, incapable of a special continued occupancy, incapable of receiving exclusively the labour of any individual person or State mixed with it, is *incapable of becoming an object of property:* that however the Authority of an usurped power of religion, however the Force of Empire, may attempt to give imaginary boundaries to the open, unbounded, undefined parts of this COMMON OCEAN, drawn by those who were as ignorant of Astronomy and Geography, as they were of the laws of Nature, as ignorant of Heaven as of Earth, boundaries which common justice never can fix, nor which common sense ever can find; it *can never become an object of dominion*; and that, therefore, the OCEAN should in policy, as it is in fact, remain common and free

Pervium cunctis iter.

If

If the Sovereigns of Europe should in this view of things conceive that the Commercial System of Europe is changing in fact, and in wisdom and policy should be changed; that the great Commerce of North America, emancipated from its provincial state, not only coincides with, but is a concurring cause of, this change; that *the present combination of these events form a crisis*, which Providence, as it were, with a more than ordinary interposition hath prepared: and that Heaven itself seems to call upon them, to whom it hath committed the interest and happiness of mankind, to co-operate with its gracious Providence: if listening to the voice of reason, who brings experience in her hand, they should be convinced that of all the fruitless follies, which rivalship of ambition, or the restless reckless activity of politics hath ever drawn them into, there is nothing so absurd as warring against each other about an object which, as it is separated from Europe, will have nothing to do with its embroils, and will not belong exclusively to any of them. If listening to this voice, which

as

as that of an Angel, announcing peace and good-will to mankind, summons them to leave off the endless useless operations of war; to consider the present crisis as an object of Council and not of War; and, therefore, to meet in communications and intercourse of their reasoning powers: surely these Sovereigns, who hold themselves to be the Vicegerents of Heaven's power on earth, will act with this its manifested spirit and will.

The maritime powers of Europe, let them continue the war to what length of time they may, must (before peace, respecting that continent, respecting America, and the mixed interests of Europe and America, can be even treated of) must convene by their Consuls, Commissioners, or other Ministers, in order to consider the several points on which the war broke out, the points in claim and in actual contest, the points on which they may safely suspend hostilities, the points which must form the basis of treaty, and which will enter into the future system, the point on which peace by that system may not only be made but
$\hspace{6em}$ established

established amongst the nations of the Atlantic ocean. Will not then reason and benevolence, in which (in this peculiar crisis) true policy and their right and best interest is included, suggest to their hearts, and actuate their Councils to convene a Congress, *before they are engaged in further hostilities,* before the devastation of war extends ruin and misery yet further. Some such measure, derived from the same feelings and reasonings, actuated by the same motives, and pointing to the same views, as led the the several great Trading Bodies of Europe to *convene in a* CONGRESS, which gave rise to the Hanseatic League, is neither contrary to, nor out of the course of public business; but is, on the other hand, what the nature of the present crisis in a more than ordinary necessity requires. In this model there is example in fact, precedents in wisdom and policy, applicable in the same manner to almost the same case as then existed. If the Statesman, who on such occasions are to advise their Sovereigns, should think that this example does not come up to the present case, or that the
mechanic

mechanic commercial reafoning of fuch homely parties can never be a model to the fublime of politics; this paper (juft obferving in the paffing, that thofe who think fo, know nothing of the wifdom of that League) would moft humbly recommend it to thefe Statefmen, taking up the fubject in an enlarged, liberal, philofophic view, to confider difpaffionately, and weigh thoroughly, *whether fome* GENERAL COUNCIL, on the model of that concerted between the great Henry of France and Elizabeth of England, two as noble fpirits and as wife politicians as the world hath fince feen, *fhould not now be propofed.* This Memoire does not mean a General Council, erected into the fame eftablifhment (although on the fame bafe) as *their defigns went to,* which was to the forming a Council of Adminiftration, for regulating and conducting *a general political fyftem* of all Europe. The general Council here fuggefted, is fimply and definedly *a Council of Commerce,* for all Europe and North America (abfolutely exclufive of all and every point of politics) formed by the feveral Sovereigns fending

their

Commiffioners or Minifters to convene, as a Chamber or Board, reprefenting the feveral commercial interefts of each State; and, on a general liberal plan and fyftem of commerce, the conjunct and confociated common intereft of All. As fuch it fhould remain a ftanding perpetual Council of deliberation and advice, and A SEAT OF JUDICIAL ADMINISTRATION common to all. *" Continuellement affemble en corps de "Senat pour deliberer fur les affaires fur- "venantes, s'occuper à difcuter les differens "interêts, pacifier les querelles, eclaircir & "vuider tous les affaires---pour affurer mu- "tuellement la liberté du commerce."* Alfo as a GREAT AND GENERAL COURT OF ADMIRALTY, to take cognizance of fuch matters of commerce in litigation, as, according to its eftablifhment, fhall come duly before it: and of all offences which fhall be committed againft thofe general and common laws of trade, which fhall have been, with ratification of the Sovereign Powers, eftablifhed by it.

Such a Council might not only prevent a moft dreadful general war, which feems to be coming on in Europe; but, if it should be so happy as to agree on such reglements as would establish peace at present, might, for ever after be the means to prevent all future occasions of war, arising from commercial quarrels. Or, if the rage of war did force itself upon the world, it would then be a Seat of common justice, open to all nations, for the relief of the peaceable, industrious, and innocent, who should be accidentally or iniquitously injured by any of the warring parties: a seat of such justice as does not exist, and cannot be expected, in any private national Court of Admiralty, in the present state of nations. Whatever is the fate of every other part of this proposition, the present entangled, confounded, vague state of the marine law of nations, seems to be such, as creates a necessity, which must draw this part into establishment. At present, all principle, rule, and law, seems to be as much lost and gone, as if the nations were fallen back to the old state of piracy, under their old barbarism. Europe cannot, even in war, go on under the present abrogation of all treaties, and all the laws of nations.

If

If the state of things, if the combination of events are, in fact, such as mark the necessity of some such General Council: If the minds and tempers of Sovereigns, whose hearts are in the hands of Providence, be in such frame as the impression of these things seems naturally to make: And if under this view of things, and in this spirit of wisdom, they should send their Commissioners or Ministers to convene in such a General Council, with powers and instructions to form some general laws and establishment on the ground of UNIVERSAL COMMERCE: the cardinal points which will most likely come under deliberation will be: 1st. How far, in right, and how far in policy, it may be best for All, to establish, on mutual agreement, the MARE LIBERUM: and how far each individual nation, (providing for the security of that peculiar property and dominion which they have, occupy, and duly hold, in local defined bays and harbours, &c. enclosed within the boundaries and coasts of their landed dominions) may accede to this establishment, as a law of nations.

2dly. How far the univerſal Jus Navigandi may be, or can be eſtabliſhed, conſiſtent with the preſent national claims of the ſeveral Maritime States; or how thoſe may be accommodated, mutually and reciprocally, ſo as to lead to ſuch eſtabliſhment hereafter. On this ground they will naturally meet each other, in forming at leaſt ſome general ſyſtem of regulations and laws, common to all, under which this univerſal commerce may act and be protected: So that the exerciſe of this right may extend whereſoever the ocean flows, and be as free as the air which wafts it over that ocean in all directions.

3dly. This will lead to deliberation on the Libertas universalis Commerciorum, free ports, and free markets, in open equal traffick.

As a concomitant meaſure, or at leaſt (theſe being ſettled) as a neceſſary conſequence of them, the Members of this Council muſt enter into convention, afterwards to be ratified by the reſpective Sovereigns, of reciprocal ſtipulations and terms, as to Port Duties and Market Tolls.

The

The adjuftment of this latter point will derive, and naturally take its form from the mode of the eftablifhment of the three former matters. They will, however, be beft and moft wifely fettled, by thofe States who are in circumftances which enable them, and who are under fuch a fpirit of wifdom as will direct them, to abolifh, by degrees, all Port Duties; and to raife their revenue by Excife, Tailles, and other internal fources of finance, as are collected not from the feller, where every impofition lays with redoubled load of tax on the Subject, and comes with defalcated and defective revenue to the State, but immediately on the confumer; where the load muft be proportioned to the abilities of his bearing it, and whence, whatever is collected, comes in full to the State. " Add to this, that it would be a means of making that country which adopted this meafure, A FREE PORT; a circumftance very defireable to every well-wifher of his country. See then whether it does not deferve the care of every worthy

patriot

patriot to make such a scheme (if it can be) feasible and practicable."*

If the State of Europe, by its circumstances and modes of business, by the spirit of its politicks, by the temper and understanding of its Sovereigns, is not yet prepared and ripe for any such general system and establishment of Universal Commerce, under the Mare Liberum, the Jus Navigandi, and the Libertas Universalis Commerciorum: The business of this Council will turn on the making of such alterations, accommodations, and reform in the old system, as may suit and follow the changes of it. They will, therefore, deliberate first, on the nature and extent of the conditional grants of privileges of trade, which, under the air of protection, they shall offer to America: Under this idea they must settle with Her and amongst each other quite new arrangements of tariffs. As they shall advance in multiplication of difficulties, and by degrees to a conviction of the impracticability of this line of measures; they

* Sir Mat. Decker.

will,

will, by degrees, raife even in their own ideas, this nation to be States admitted, and next go upon the experiment of treaties of commerce with her, on the old European fyftem. Experience will teach them, that this will create a rivalfhip, which will evade and break all treaties of commerce. Here then will they come round in a circle to the point of neceffity, as herein before ftated, which, firft or laft, muft force into eftablifhment, the meafure defcribed in this paper. † *Voila tout ce qu' on peut raifonablement exiger, Il n' eft au pouvoir de l' humanité, que de preparer et agir. Le Succes eft l' Ouvrage d' une main plus puiffante.*

† Duc de Sulli, Liv. 30.

ADVERTISEMENT.

THE following Paper ſtates and explains the Syſtem of the New World in America; the natural Liberty of the Individual ſettled there; the Frame into which the Communities of individuals (prior to all conſideration of Political Society) naturally form themſelves. By theſe principles it leads to the diſcuſſion of the nature of their States and their political Freedom; of the nature of the Confederation and General Government; and from hence the Spirit and Temper of Polity, which may hereafter form *the Reaſon of State,* or Syſtem of Adminiſtration in the affairs of that Empire, are ſketched out.

As the several matters which range under this general Subject are intimately interwoven with the *Essence*, and deeply interest the *Existence* of this Sovereign Empire, they ought to be apparent to, and to be understood by, every Citizen of America, who has a share in the business of his Country: this Memorial, therefore, is addressed to the SOVEREIGNS OF AMERICA. It is, moreover, published to the Citizens at large, as " *What concerns All, should be considered of by All.*"

A practical knowledge of the matters contained in this Paper, especially of those points which respect the *new System* of a New World; a knowledge of the *Constitution* of the General Government, and of the ground and
move-

movements of the American *Administration*, is indispensably necessary to every Statesman in Europe, who may have Connections and Habits of business with this New Empire: this Paper is therefore published to Europe at large.

It is not written for the Reading, nor calculated to the Reasoning of British Politicians: it is drawn by a Scale below such Sublimity: its home-spun reasonings will be unintelligible to British Statesmen. A few Copies, however, are reserved for the inferior class of Readers and Reasoners who will understand the Memorialist.

If He could flatter himself that the Statesmen and Politicians of Great-Britain would descend from their

their Superior Regions, and condefcend to caſt an Eye, or rather a Thought, on ſuch a trifling Paper of ſuch an unexperienced Theoriſt as the Memorialiſt; He has only to caution them againſt *patching* their politics with the only *remnant-rag* of their folly that ſticks to their backs, viz. *an Idea that an* UNION *with America, or ſome part of it,* is *practicable and politic.* This propoſition, *framed into a meaſure,* is the only one left to compleat, beyond redemption, the Ruin of this Country.

A MEMORIAL

ADDRESSED TO THE

SOVEREIGNS of AMERICA.

HAVING prefumed to addrefs to the Sovereigns of Europe a Memorial, ftating,

1ft, The Combination of Events, as they ftood in fact and operation between the Old and New Worlds, between Europe and America:

2dly, Marking the train of confequences which muft have been the Effect of this combination, and which is in part arifen into Event by the Eftablifhment of the Sovereignty of the American States;

3dly,

3dly, and laſtly, Suggeſting what that ſpirit of Policy, and marking what that line of Conduct ought to be, with which *the advancing State* of things ſhould be met:

Permit me now to addreſs this Memorial to You Sovereigns of America. I ſhall not addreſs you with the Court-titles of Gothic Europe, nor with thoſe of ſervile Aſia. I will neither addreſs your Sublimity or Majeſty, your Grace or Holineſs, your Eminence or Highmightineſs, your Excellence or Honours. What are Titles, where Things themſelves are known and underſtood? What Title did the Republick of Rome take? The State was known to be Sovereign, and the Citizens to be Free. What could add to this Glory? * Therefore, United States

---

* If it were neceſſary for the American States to take a Stage-name in the Diplomatic Drama of Politics; to aſſume for their Title of Addreſs ſome *noun ſubſtantive* expreſſive of the Spirit and Virtue which is ſuppoſed peculiarly to reſide in them;

STATES AND CITIZENS OF AMERICA, I addrefs You, as You are; I do it under every fenfe and fentiment of Reverence to Your SOVEREIGN STATION; and under a confcious fenfe of the diftance of my own private one. And yet, from the relation which I have formerly borne to the States, both when † I ferved them under their command,

them; I would addrefs myfelf to THEIR FREE-DOMS. This is the peculiar gift of Heaven; this is the Spirit of their Caufe and Eftablifhment. Be this their Holinefs, their Grace, their Excellence, their Honour: be this their Polity, and they will eftablifh the Majefty of the American Union, and will rife into high and mighty States.

† The firft Public Commiffion that this Memorialift held, the firft of his honours, an honour which he efteems as highly as any that he hath ever fince enjoyed, was that of being Commiffioner fent from the Province, now the State Maffachufett's-Bay, to negotiate an Union of the Forces of Pennfylvania, New-Jerfey, and New-York, with the Forces of New-England, in an expedition againft Crown-Point, in which negotiation he fucceeded, and which expedition gave the firft turn to the fate of the War of 1755. He began his courfe by learning to ferve them, and he afterwards fo commanded as to obtain the approbation of thofe where he governed, and the honourable teftimony they bore him. Afterwards, in the private ftation to which he was configned in

his

command, and after when I commanded —I addrefs You in the confcioufnefs of fomething above ‡ a Subject, in that of a Citizen. I addrefs you not only as SOVEREIGN States, eftablifhed and acknowledged; I congratulate You as FREE States, as founded on and built up in the Principles of Political Freedom. I congratulate Human Nature that it hath pleafed God to eftablifh an Afylum to which Men of all Nations who wifh for

his native land, he invariably endeavoured to ferve the Caufe of Freedom and Peace; he had the means and took the occafion to become an *efficient fpring*, though not permitted to be *the Inftrument* of Peace. Born in that part of his Nation which inhabits Great-Britain, but having been employed as a Political agent only within that part which poffeffes America, he efteems himfelf, politically fpeaking, a *Citizen* of America, though by birth a *Subject* of Great-Britain.

‡ I derive my diftinction from the Romans: I adopt the precedent from the Commiffioners Plenipotentiary of America. The Romans fay, *Non in regno Populum Rom. fed in Libertate effe:* and the Commiffioners, with the moft exact precifion, mark, in the provifional Treaty with Great-Britain, the characteriftic of thofe who are *in regno*, and of thofe who are *in libertate*, by this expreffion, the " *Subjects* of the one, and the *Citizens* of the other."

and

and deserve Freedom may fly, and under which they may find Refuge. In the contemplation of this wish, and in the view of this general happiness to mankind, depending on your establishment, I presume to address this Memorial to You.

Accept with gracious interpretation and condescension my Apology. I feel that it would be an impertinent assumption, nay, that it would be ridiculous, were I to presume to advise the States in the course and practice of Government. The free Citizens of America, whose practice from their youth is in the business of their Township, of their County, of their Country; whose discipline and whole education, whose character, is in constant training to the knowledge and exercise of Government and its powers; will in their reasoning prove more reasonable, in their actions more efficient, and in their political conduct wiser and more *au fait* in the affairs of their *new world* than the first Statesmen of Europe, who have acted on the ſtage of the *old one*. A free Citizen, participant of the Sovereignty of his State, who learns and is practiſed in rotation of offices, both to ſerve and to command, feels by habit in his mind, as he doth in his animal frame, almoſt mechanically, and without adverting to the reaſon at the time, the meaſure and the movement which every ſurrounding circumſtance calls for. The character, thus acquired, creates in the *reaſoning* Agent the ſelf-conſcious feel of its natural energy: as the habits of exerciſe in the body give to the *moving* Agent the animal feel of ſelf-poiſe. In taking, however, a new ſtation, in ſtanding amidſt new and unexperienced relations, the Agent feels the center of his animal poiſe removed; he feels ſomewhat that did not make part of his former ſelf-conſciouſneſs: he is, for a time, as it were, on a conſtrained Balance of Mind and Body. In this ſituation he finds and feels, that not old habits, but new exertions of diſcernment; a ſpirit of inveſtiga-

investigation and induction; an analysing Spirit applied to new matter, not a compounding judgment on the old, must come forth and act. Under circumstances important, in situations pregnant like these, the American Politician and Statesman, whose training and practice is in a course of experiments, as in the new philosophy, will not refuse to hear any advice which is suggested, will not reject the offers of any service, though he neither calls for the one nor wants the other. Making his experiences in every line of reasoning, in that of others as well as his own, he will frame and found his own resolutions on his own reasons so informed.

The Scite and Circumstances into which your Affairs were brought in the year 1776: and your self-consciousness prompting you to find that you were not *in fact* what political establishments had made you *by law*, a Branch of a family, subject to and dependent on another Branch of the same family as your Sovereigns; but that you were what nature had wrought you up to, equal brothers of the fame family: feeling yourfelves driven by neceffity to a feparation " from the political Bands " which had hitherto connected you, You " found it neceffary to affume, amongft " the Powers of the earth, that Separate, " and Equal Station to which the laws of " Nature and of Nature's God intitled " you : and therefore Declared, that the " United Colonies of Britons in America, " were and of right ought to be, FREE " and INDEPENDENT STATES."

This, like all other revolutions of Nations, hath been contefted by arms. *Sweet Love changing its nature turns to bittereft hate*; fevere therefore and deftructive has been the war of Brethren. The appeal was to Heaven : and the fuccefs of your Caufe is a proof in fact, that the vigour of natural principles muft always in the end prove impregnable and irrefiftible to mere force, however fupported : That a Syftem of meafures founded in the nature of

things,

things, and actuated by the direct rule of Common Sense, must always rise superior to and overtop all establishments founded in the devices of Men, and built up in all the Art and Mystery of Politics: That a Conscious Spirit, which such circumstances inspire, will bear up against and finally bear down all artificial courage of Military Power, howsoever trained and strengthened: That a Cause so founded, so animated, so conducted, will predominate and be established. It hath been the decided will of God, that this your Cause should prevail, and that your Independence and Sovereignty should be acknowledged by the Sovereigns of the earth, now your equals.

As I recommended in my Memorial to the Sovereigns of Europe; so in this now addressed to the * MAJESTY OF THE PEOPLE

---

* This expression, which the Memorialist will have frequent occasion to repeat, is justified in the precedent of the forms used in expressing the Sovereignty of the Roman People, as used in some of their Treaties;

People of America, the whole argument recommends to their confideration, 1. What the precife change of their Syftem is. 2. What may be the general confequences of fuch change. 3. With what fpirit, and by what conduct *the advancing ftate of things* fhould be met. The inveftigation of thefe points can be purfued only by that felf-collected frame of mind within yourfelves, combined with a plain and fober love of Truth, which will confider well *of what fpirit you are*; which will ftate Perfons and Things *as they really exift*; and will, in the right Spirit of Sovereigns of a State founded in Political Freedom, treat them *as being what they are*.

The moment that you became, *de jure* by the Law of Nations, acknowledged independent and Sovereign, equal to other Sovereigns

Treaties; Majeftatem Populi Rom. comitèr confervent: and as a common form in their acts of Government; Fit Senatûs Confultum, ut Imperium Populi Rom. Majeftafq; confervaretur. *Cicer. pro Rabirio.*

Sovereigns of the earth, and having no reference but to yourfelves, was the moment of your greateft difficulty and danger. I have, with an anxious zeal for the liberties of mankind, confidered thefe difficulties and this danger; and it will be one purpofe of this Memorial, to ftate them, firft as they refpect the exiftence, next as they refpect the Conftitution of this Sovereign.

This moment will fhow whether the States and Citizens of America are capable of eftablifhing and of permanently maintaining this independent Sovereignty; are capable of actuating in truth and fact this fpirit of political Freedom, firft, as it derives from yourfelves; fecondly, as it may depend upon your Leaders; and laftly, as this fpirit and this eftablifhment may be affected by thofe Foreign Powers with whom as neighbours, with whom as Guarantees, with whom as friends by alliances, this Exiftence ftands connected.

It hath pleafed God to eftablifh your Sovereignty

Sovereignty by the force of arms; it hath pleafed him to fix the rights of your equal ftation with the Sovereigns of the earth in the rights of Treaty, and that your Empire fhould be acknowledged by the Law of Nations: He hath, however, fo wrought, according to the ufual difpenfations of his providence, that you muft work out your own falvation. If you are not in your *Principles*, in your *Spirit*, in the *State of your Confederation*, in the *Conftitution* of your General Government, in the *Powers of your Union*, as yet ripe for Political Freedom and formed for Empire; * your Liberty is immature, your Sovereignty is premature. The firft danger is, if you miftake your Spirit, if you neglect to build on your real foundation, as it is laid in Nature, or if you raife a fuperftructure not confonant to it. Examine, therefore,

---

* Neque ambigitur quin Brutus, qui tantum gloriæ, Superbo exacto Rege, meruit; peffimo publico id facturus fuerit, fi libertatis immaturæ cupidine priorum Regum alicui Regnum extorfiffet.
Liv.

therefore, of what Spirit you are: Search thoroughly and survey the Ground that is the foundation of your General Constitution, and, attending soberly in reason, and not in the partial unequal movements of passion, distinguish the operations of Polity which arise by the energy of natural principles, from those which are forced on by art, and constrained by violence against Nature. Follow those principles in the order of your Superstructure: and when the great Machine of Government is formed, actuate it by the Spirit of Freedom as it lies in Truth. Feel, as one soul, the concentered Vigour of Sovereign *Imperium:* feel the self-poize of your natural Station, the Center and balance of your Force; the course and range of your organised energy; the Spring of Activity in your political person: and you will find it no difficult matter to stand firm on the Basis of your Sovereignty: You will experience but little obstruction, at least such as is of little consequence to the exercise and adminiſtration of your *Imperium*. You will feel the meanwhile the expanding powers of your Liberties and Freedom come forward, by a natural vitality, into Fruit, the fruits of Peace, Plenty, and the ſolid permanent happineſs of Being.

Theſe are not words of courſe, this is not mere harangue: thoſe who knew the States and Citizens of America, as it was my duty to do, and as I did, ſaw, not from an *ex poſt facto* view of the Effect as it is now decided, but in the operation of the Cauſes working to this certain effect, and pronounced, not in vague and general terms of harangue, but in defined ſpecific declarations of leading Facts, that Ye were ripe for Political Freedom; that the foundation of a great Empire was laid; and that it would ariſe into Eſtabliſhment. And thus this your Memorialiſt, in his Memorial addreſſed to the Sovereigns of Europe, ſtated you.

That you have united, at the riſque of every

every thing which forms the happiness and exiſtence of Man, to oppoſe the Meaſures and *Provincial* Government of your late Sovereign: that you have perſevered in your reſiſtance to the emancipating of Yourſelves from all regal Power: that you have taken the Government into your own hands:* that you have conducted it with ſuch ſpirit through ſo many difficulties and dangers in war, and in treaties, is no unequivocal demonſtration to all mankind, that the ſpirit of freedom and a right ſenſe of Government dwells in the Citizens of America. If, when theſe Citizens come to the forming of the political eſtabliſhment of their General Government, an uniform Idea of Self-eſtimation (each aiming to be that, and no more, than he really is, and all treating

---

* Non inopiæ Ærarii, non vis hoſtium, non adverſa res ingentem eorum animum ſubegit, quin, quod virtute ceperant, ſimul cum animo retinerent. Atq; ea magis fortibus conciliis quam bonis præliis patrata ſunt. *Salluſtius* ſic ſcribit de ortu et progreſſu Rom. Imperii.

each other invariably as what he is in his individuality) actuates the People; if a temper that equalizes every participant of the Community in the rank and order in which he is a Member of the State, actuates the body of the People; if a jealous guard over the rights, property, lives, and security of the People, interwoven with a conscious Reverence for the Honour of Government; if a heartfelt duty, active in the support of Government, combined with a prompt and active spirit of resistance to every thing which would obstruct or abate its operations, forms the character of the Americans: if this spirit animating the body of the people, actuates their leaders; the State, bottomed on the real and actual foundation as it lies in the Community, will be built up in its Constitution conformable to it;* and the Power of the Govern-

---

* The reasons why the American Empire will not be liable to the division of interests, and to the

Government and the Spirit of the People will conspire in the Administration of it. This power and Spirit so combined pervades the whole in its reasoning part, and gives spring to the whole in every act of Government. It equally exists in the passive virtue of Obedience, as in the active duty of Command. Liberty will feel the conscious sense of confidence and uniform obedience; and Government, governing by the lead of the People, will command irresistibly. There can be no contention for, nor acquisition of, unequal Domination in Men; but the Contest will be (so it was at Rome in her happier days) who shall best promote the interest and honour of the State in serving, or best exert it in governing. On the contrary, where there is a reluctance in the Individual, arising partly from a want of entire assurance in himself and his political situation, and partly from a jealousy

---

the ruinous contests which took place in Rome, will be given by the Memorialist in that part which considers the Constitution.

of those in other situations, to establish such power as is necessary to render the State AN AGENT ; where there is a resistance to the command of all above, and a desire of Domination over all below; where there is an impatience opposing itself reciprocally to all command on one hand, and to all check and restraint of power on the other; where that temper operates in the People, or actuates their Leaders, and is mistaken for the Spirit of Liberty : either the State is not founded on the true basis of the People ; or is not built up in its constitution according to the Frame of the Community ; or there does not reside the true and genuine spirit of Liberty in the Community, operating to Political freedom in the State. Let the Citizens of America therefore enter seriously and in earnest with themselves into the enquiry : Whether they find within their Community a Spirit of Attraction operating, as an internal principle, to Union; or whether their Community

munity has been compreſſed into its preſent Confederation only by an external cauſe, and will remain ſo compreſſed ſo long as, and only ſo long as, that power ſhall act upon them from without. Thoſe who, at the time of the commencement of theſe events, knew the character of that People, and watched their conduct, knew that the vigour of natural Principles drew them to reſiſt the unnatural violence of *Provincial* Government. This Vigour of natural Principles gave Unity, Wiſdom, and perſevering firmneſs to their Councils; and the ardour of the Spirit of Liberty gave ſtrength to their own arms, and rendered them impregnable to thoſe of the Enemy. If, examining the temper and ſpirit of the people, and the Conduct of their Leaders, they find that the ſame principles continue now to operate from an internal attraction when all external compreſſive cauſes are removed; if the ſame ſpirit of liberty continues to act, in a perfect reciprocity of thoſe rights, which

each

each individual, according to the frame of the community, is entitled to; if the collective Spirit of thefe Sources has a direct tendency to form into political freedom, to which all are ready to facrifice; the Citizens of America may be confident *that their Liberty is Mature*. They may and will eftablifh the Sovereignty of their States, and the United General Government as Independent and in Freedom.

The train of events, extraordinary as they have been, hath eftablifhed their *Imperium*, and by the Law of Nations they are acknowledged to be, *de jure* as well as *de facto*, SOVEREIGNS. A fecond line of confideration, therefore, parallel to the former, leads to the enquiry, What the genuine *Spirit of Sovereignty* is, and whether it exifts as a *political Pinciple* in the Community, is combined with the Conftitution as a Vital principle of the State, and actuates the adminiftration of the ge-tal Government.

If the fpirit of Liberty, in a people founded

founded as a ſtate in political freedom, and built up in a Superſtructure conſonant to the actual frame of the community, inſpires that people with a ſenſe of its own ſecurity in that foundation, and therefore animates it with that confidence which ſuch principles give : that People will feel, that, as They at large are repreſented by their elected Delegates, ſo is the Majeſty of the People repreſented by, and reſides in, the Sovereignty, which they have eſtabliſhed. They will repoſe themſelves in this as their Palladium ; and will, as Participants and Conſtituents of the State, truſt and give full Confidence to the Supreme Officer or Officers, whether permanent or changing in rotation, who adminiſters and executes that Office, whoſe Honour, Dignity, Power, and * Amplitude,

---

* This word AMPLITUDO, as uſed by the Romans, is included under the general Idea MAJESTAS, and means pretty nearly the ſame, or ſomething ſimilar to our Engliſh word *Prerogative*. As that word has been applied to a Monarchy, I have

E   adopted

tude, is the Reprefentative of this Majefty.

The Word *Sovereign* is a Gothic Feudal term; it precifely meant the Supreme *Command paramount* over all other fubordinate Commands, where thofe commands, however, were fovereign within their own jurifdiction. It is *Super-regnum inter regna minora.* I hope, whereever in this Memorial I ufe this Term, to be underftood according to the ftrict definition of the word *Majeftas,* ufed by the Roman State, as the collective idea under which are included and refide *the Jura, Imperia, Fafces, Dignitas, Poteftas et Amplitudo Populi Americani.* Under this

---

adopted in this Tract the term which the Romans ufed under a Popular Government, meaning a *Fulnefs of Power,* which fhould not, in all cafes, be defined; and is beft held without definition, fo as to exert itfelf in all cafes *pro Salute Populi*; but which is yet effectually limited where that people, thinking it hath unnecefarily adopted, or in its exertions exceeded *that Lex Suprema,* interpofes to check it. Majeftas eft Amplitudo & Dignitas Civitatis. *Cic. de Orat.* 113. Majeftatem minuit qui Amplitudinem Civitatis detrimento afficit. *Cic. ad Heren.*

Idea,

Idea, and under this definition of Sovereignty, the Memorial proceeds to enquire whether there doth actually exist in America *that Majesty of the People* under which, and within which, the rights and liberties, the power and prerogative, the honour and dignity of the States and Citizens are collectively concentered: and *whether this is actually so established as to be the efficient Government.*

If a right Sense of this Spirit of Sovereignty, thus established in, and combined with, political freedom, pervades the feeling of the people; is conscious that the collected information and reason of the whole concenters in this Majesty; that the combined Force of the whole springs from this Center of Power and activity; this sense will dwell in the opinion of the people with all that esteem for the wisdom of the *Imperium*, that respect to its Authority, that veneration of its Honour and Dignity, and that *Consensus obedientium* under its power, which

alone

alone forms the principle of the Sovereignty (I had rather fay) the Majefty of the People as free Citizens. On this principle they will eftablifh this Majefty with fuch powers as are neceffary to give it efficiency; for not to feel that they may venture to give full fcope and efficient powers to it, is to doubt of the foundation of their own Freedom, is to withhold the real eftablifhment, while they fet up an Idol with which to Mock themfelves. They will rather give it fuch AMPLITUDE of power as may enable it, in all cafes, not defined and not definable, to fecure and promote the *Salus Populi.*

Sovereigns as they are, and are declared to be by the Sovereigns of the Earth their Equals, if they do not form one general Efficient *Imperium* as the Political Center of the Union, as Reprefentative of the Majefty of the whole Sovereign Confederation; as the executive fpring of felf-motion and Force in the State; the Liberty, Independence, and Sovereignty of the
feveral

several States, will prove exactly such as T. Q. Flaminius, by order of the Roman Senate, affected to restore and to give to the States of Greece; or such as the policy of the same Senate directed Paulus Æmilius to form the four Free and Independent Democracies of Macedonia upon —so independent as to have no alliance of Polity, or intercommunion of Trade with each other. This Memorial will not enter into the detail of this adduced example: for if the reading of the History is not sufficient to awaken a jealous sense of this Situation, Reason will but more tire and deaden that Sense. All, therefore, that will be here done is to recommend to the serious contemplation of the American States, to compare in those examples the measures taken, and the events which succeeded, to their own situation, in an anxious looking to future events. This is said in excess of caution: but One may hope that it is totally unnecessary. If the Memorialist is not mistaken in his

idea

idea of the free People of America, He should rather think they will cloath it with such Honours and Dignity, that its Authority rather than its power may be seen, and be willingly submitted to: but they will yet arm it with such Powers as shall maintain the *Imperium*, and bear down all unconstitutional recoil against it.

If this genuine Spirit pervades the character of the People, those amongst them, whom the Sense and Opinion of the People destine to be Rulers, will be trained to the character of Sovereigns, and, when actually cloathed with the Majesty of the People, will feel a consciousness, not of the pride of their own person, but of the Honour and Dignity of the People. Under this conscious sense they will, as the Consuls of Rome did, act the Character of Sovereigns in a higher tone of dignity than Kings and Princes, whose conscious feel of Majesty is centered in their own narrow Selves. They will act

with

with less pride, but more commanding ascendency; with less violence, but with greater effect; with less Craft, but with more Wisdom; with Truth, Honour, and the real Spirit of Majesty.

If this Spirit of Sovereignty does not reside in the People; if, through defect of this, the State is not formed to act as a Sovereign with all the Majesty of the People; this New Sovereign may, like a Meteor in its rapid trajectory, blaze in the Heavens, and astonish the Earth for a time, but will not be found in any uniform revolving orbit, nor become established as a permanent System.

> Ostendent terris hunc tantum, Fata neq; ultra Esse sinent.

On the contrary, if they find within the Community the Self-spring of Government; if they are conscious that they have formed their *Imperium* in this Spirit, and not in the Spirit of Domination; if they have established their Government, as in political Freedom, so in Amplitude of of Majesty, the Spirit of Heaven will answer their call, and inspire their cause. "*I have become,*" it saith, "*a glorious diadem to the remnant of the People: 1. Arise, ascend thy high seat: 2. Cloath thyself with thy power: 3. Lift up on high thy Standard to the Nations.*" Establish your Sovereign Government; Cloath it with the Majesty of the People; and claim, insist on, and maintain, in all its amplitude, the honour and dignity of this Sovereign Majesty with all the Sovereigns of the Earth.

Having examined the nature of the *Spirit of Liberty*, the nature of the *Spirit of Sovereignty*, as forming, when combined in the natural principles of a People, the *Essence* of efficient Government founded in freedom,—this Memorial proceeds to the examination of those relative matters which may, both internally and externally, affect the *Existence* of that Free and Independent Sovereign.

A newly-established State viewed

under the circumſtances of its Birth, and with reference to thoſe relations amongſt which it muſt, in its firſt years, take its courſe, will be ſeen to ſtand in the ſame predicament at its firſt eſtabliſhment, as Man, the Individual, doth at his birth. Cicero, in treating of the beſt poſſible Republic, takes his ground of reaſoning from this reference: "*Homo non ut a Matre, ſed a Novercâ -Naturâ editus eſt in vitam ; corpore nudo & fragili & infirmo; animo autem anxio ad moleſtias, humili ad timores, molli ad labores, prono ad libidines, in quo tamen ineſt tanquam obrutus quidem divinus ignis ingenii & mentis.*"

It hath not, however, been ſo with the American States at this their coming forth. They have been in their infancy nurtured and protected by nature as by a mother, between whom and her children there has been the pureſt reciprocation of maternal affection and filial Piety, until evil councils broke the tie. Under this relation theſe

these States arose to manhood : all, therefore, which Cicero refers to in his allusion to the birth or first establishment of a Republic, *de corpore nudo & fragili & infirmo; de animo anxio ad molestias, humili ad timores, molli ad labores*; all that he refers to as to the wants, defects, infirmities, and weaknesses, of Infancy, doth not apply, either in mind or body, to those States adult in manhood, before they took their station of Independence. * " *They are already hardened into Republics.*" They are come forth in full maturity of age. It is however at an age *prona ad libidines*.

As man in his youth lives under a perpetual conflict of his passions; so have all States, so will the States of America, at their first emancipation to liberty, feel, in the effervescent temper of their youth, the same tumults in the bosom of the State:

* This is an expression of the Earl of Clarendon in the MS. draught of his plan for sending Commissioners to America in 1664.

* they cannot therefore too carefully watch over their hearts, that, while they think that they are cultivating the sacred Love of Liberty, they may not become inflamed with the libidinous passion of Licence. They must in their zeal for the interest of the state, in their exertions of their constitutional share of power in the government, in their natural and not inuseful differings of opinion upon men and measures, keep a constant check over the ardour of young impressions; otherwise that which should be the natural (I had almost said the mechanical) motion of their agency, will break out in the conflicts of

---

* What is here said of the *Libidines adolescentis Civitatis* is not the refinement of Theory and inexperience, but the repeated lesson of the greatest and most experienced Statesmen: and in the very manner in which I have here given the caution against those political *libidines*, Cicero gives the like caution in his sixth book de Repub. Graves enim dominæ cogitationum libidines, infinita quædam cogant atq; imperant, quæ quia expleri atq; satiari nullo modo possunt, ad omne facinus impellunt eos qui illecebris suis incenduntur.

parties and factions, perpetually tending to establish the interests and domination of men. *Et hæc quasi materies omnium malorum semper fuere.* The lead of America will, by combinations of military subordination, tend in a direct line to the despotism of One; or, by civil intrigues, and the corruption of the purse, converge in oblique lines to the Tyranny of the Few; or, by the energy of enterprizing ambition, be wrought into a discordant and repulsive state, which will break all order and dissolve all system. Had this been the case in Rome, *Dissipatæ* (saith Livy) *Res, nondum adultæ, discordiâ forent, quas fovit tranquilla moderatio imperii, eoque nutriendo perduxit, ut bonam frugem libertatis, maturis jam viribus, ferre possent.* May the same sense of Liberty and Government in the People, the same *tranquilla moderatio imperii* in their Leaders, warm and animate the Spirit of America! And may that spirit, ardent yet moderated; that Government, though active,

active, yet not violent; bring forth the fruits of Empire founded in political Freedom, for the protection, peace, and happinefs, of mankind, in one portion at leaft of this Earth.

This Memorial hath ftated and explained the operation of the internal felf-working Principle, as the fiift caufe of union in Community, which by one common energy of univerfal attraction creates (as in nature by natural principles) one common center, to which the feveral energies of each and all tend and confpire. If human nature, and a community of human beings, could be found perfect as to reafon, truth, and wifdom; not to be perverted by paffions; not to be feduced and corrupted by vicious affections; this attractive principle would alone be efficient to the End of union in Government. This is not the cafe; God hath therefore been pleafed to fuperadd another caufe, arifing from the very defects and depravations of man, which operates from with-

without. This compresses men against their repulsive fears and jealousies of each other, against the repellant temper which frauds, dissentions, violence, and attempts at domination, raise amongst them by a still stronger compulsive power into closer contact, and mutual alliance for common defence. It is happy for a State, especially for a newly-established State, when this external cause continues to act; and acts to one and the same end in aid of the internal principle.

It is, on the other hand, an unfortunate and dangerous crisis to young and rising States, if the external compressive cause, which hath been found useful to a State, by rendering internal peace and union necessary, and hath been in that line of efficiency applied as part of the political System, ceases to act. While the Persians meditated or made invasions upon Greece, the several states adhered zealously and most carefully to their confederacy; but in less than fifty years after

after Xerxes was defeated and driven from Greece, the repellant spirit began to show itself in the strife of unequal interest, and in attempts of some to create a Domination over the rest; and issued in the Peloponnesian war, to the total devastation of the Country, and almost to the destruction of the States. In like manner, while neighbour nations of Italy, hostile to Rome, acted upon the State of that City as this compressive cause from without, the wisdom of its Statesmen applied the effect to the restraining and bounding the repellant principle of Discord within. These were at length removed either by conquest or alliances; yet Carthage, the rival of Rome, and upon the Sea the ascendent power, restrained the Conduct of the Citizens of Rome to the necessity of keeping the same guard upon the spirit of Dissention. *Sed quum Carthago, æmula Imperii Romani, ab stirpe interiit, Cuncta maria Terræq; patebant; Fortuna sævire & miscere omnia cœpit.*

Qui labores, pericula, dubias atq; asperas res facilè toleraverant, Iis otium divitiæ, optandæ aliis, oneri miseriæq; fuere. Igitur primò pecuniæ, dein imperii cupido crevit, &c. In like manner, now that the *Imperium* of Great Britain resides no longer within the Empire of the United States; now that the British Nation is removed from within the Dominion of those States; now that the States dwell almost alone on their great Continent, and are absolutely the Ascendent Power there; if the true *spirit of liberty,* as above described, and the *genuine spirit of Government,* does not act by the internal attractive principle of Union strongly and permanently in proportion as the external compressing cause of confederation is removed, the Americans will experience the same Fate and Fortune, and be driven, by the same miseries, to the same ruinous distress which the States of Greece and the city of Rome had wretched experience of.

It is, however, peculiarly happy for

the American States, whatever be the force and temper of this internal principle with them; that an external compreffive caufe is not wholly taken off. When they confider the difficulties which they will have to render *the line of Frontiers* between their Empire and the Britifh Provinces in America a *line of Peace*; when they experience in fact and practice the difficulties of preferving it as fuch; when they fpeculate upon the almoft numberlefs, and, at prefent, namelefs, fources of difpute and contention, which may break out between them and Spain; when, in the cool hours of unimpaffioned reflection, they begin to be apprized of the danger of their very * Alliances; they will fee that this compreffive caufe does not ceafe to act. Every friend to their peace, liberty, and happinefs, muft hope that they will fo fee it, that their States-

---

* Guaranties have a right to interpofe, and may affume a right of becoming *Arbitrers*.

men may attend to improve the effects of its operation, and to profit of this bitter but saving providence. If they improve the feelings which the States will from time to time experience of danger to the interest of the General *Imperium* from external force, so as to work the impression, which fears of that external power creates, to a permanent habit of union and confederation, as a principle of their Empire, never to be remitted, diminished, or departed from for a moment, * these States will derive internal Union and Stability to their Government from those very dangers, or the fears of those dangers, which threaten it. If, on the other

---

* This was the invariable Policy of the Patricians and Senate in the early days of Rome. Similem annum priori Consules habent. Seditiosa initia bello deinde externo tranquilla. Ea res maturam jam seditionem ac propè erumpentem repressit. *Liv.* l. ii. § 63 & 64. Bono fuisse Romanis adventum eorum constabat; orientemq; jam seditionem inter Patres & Plebem metu tam propinqui belli compressam. Lib. vii. § 12.

hand, it should unfortunately become the system of their Politics, that, divided into parties, each ascendant party of the time should, by reference to, and the interposition of, those external powers, aim to strengthen *their own* interest; the state may retain its sovereign Station; but their own Rulers will scarcely be the Sovereigns: the Reason of State will be no longer its own reason; and its Liberty will, even while it seems to act in all its forms, be bound down by the predestination of External Powers. The several States, or several Parties in the States, instead of coalescing by one uniform general attraction to the common center, will become like the blood of life in a fever, clotted into partial diseased coagulations of faction, having the most violent repulsion amongst each other. This Memorial will not enter into this topic further than to recommend to the Citizens of America, not only to read, but to compare, with what may be their own eventual cafe, the effect of this sort of reference, as it shewed itself amongst the States of Italy during the time that Rome and Carthage were Rival Powers in that country. *Unus velut morbus invaserat omnes Italiæ Civitates, ut Plebs ab Optimatibus diffentirent: Senatus Romanis faveat; Plebs ad Pænos rem traherent.* † The same malady seized the States of Greece. Factious within themselves, the Minor Party had reference to foreign interest, and sought to strengthen each their own Faction by the aid of the enemies of their Government. They applied first to the Persian Grand Monarch; in the next period, to Athens and Lacedæmon alternately, as the Aristocratic or Democratic Faction prevailed. This also well deserves the consideration of the United States of America, as to the point of reference which future parties amongst them may make to foreign aid, to French or British Power.

* Livy. † Thucydides.

This

This Memorial might here enlarge on this topic of foreign politics, as they may train between Great Britain and the United States: it would be a needlefs prefumption, fo far as refpects the American Statefman; and would not, I am fure, as nothing of the kind ever yet has been, be of any ufe to Britifh Statefmen. It might enlarge on this fubject as it refpects the States with reference to their intercourfe with Spain; their Alliance with France; their Treaties with the United Belgic States and * other powers: but, perhaps, the Statefmen of America, under the impreffions and predilections of their newly-formed friendfhips, may think the eventual State of things, which it would defcribe, to be vifionary and *en l'air*, and may hold the confiderations thereupon, which it would recommend, as the mere

---

* The Memorial will mention in another place Indian Politics, as they refpect this new Empire of America.

theoretic

theoretic essays of an unemployed and inexperienced man. This Memorial, therefore, will only repeat what the Memorial addressed to the Sovereigns of Europe stated as a maxim (rather a fundamental Principle) of American Politics: "That
" as Nature hath separated her from Eu-
" rope, and hath established her alone
" (as a Sovereign) on a great Continent,
" far removed from the Old world and all
" its embroiled interests, * that it is con-
" trary to the nature of her existence, and
" consequently to her interest, that she
" should have any connexions of Politics
" with Europe other than merely com-
" mercial; that she should be a FREE
" PORT to all Europe at large, and in
" reciprocity claim a FREE MARKET in
" Europe; and that she should have no
" commercial treaties with any European
" Power partial to such power and ex-
" clusive to others; but that she should

* Common Sense.

" give

" give and enjoy a free Navigation and an open trade with all."

Fundamental Principles fimilar to thefe, although they may not have been able to prevent her from forming fome connexions, fome alliances, may yet, if a fyftem of Politics is founded on them as decided maxims of State, and invariably and uniformly purfued, preferve her from the entanglements in which fhe might be otherwife involved, and guard her againft the dangers which the confequences of thofe connexions may lead to. Although a bold and daring, or a lucky ftroke, may fucceed for the hour or the feafon, or in the tranfient fmall affairs of Individuals; yet *nothing but Syftem*, as it arifes from the nature of the State, *will be efficient* to any permanent purpofe; to an Empire nothing but fyftem, even in the line of defence, will guard a State againft, and repel the attacks of Fortune. The moft daring Fortitude, the moft active courage, unlefs it hath fuch foundation, would become

come folly and madness, and only ruin a State with more *eclat*. There is something in Fortune which mixes itself in all Human affairs, and which perplexes and obstructs, if it does not actually command, Events. Fortune, although generally considered as an operation of chance, is not, and cannot be, any thing else but the ordinary course of natural and human events. It is a Combination arising from remote or hidden causes, from circumstances unobserved, from influences not understood, from innumerable and imperceptible *minutiæ*, which yet, combined, are causes equal to every effect that is produced. These remote, hidden, and imperceptible causes are not, and indeed scarce ever can be, considered by men : the effects, therefore, are in Event before the causes are seen, if they are ever seen afterward. Fortune, therefore, (as men usually express themselves,) mixes itself in all human affairs, and generally commands. The acutest foresight, the
firmest

firmeſt ſpirit, if acting and exerted *only on the occaſion*, can neither guard againſt nor reſiſt its Force.

<blockquote>Quid Quiſq; vitet, nunquam Homini ſatis Cautum eſt in horas.</blockquote>

No temporary reaſoning, no temporizing State-craft, applied only to *occaſions*, can either be aware of or prevent her ſtrokes; nor will the moſt inexhauſtible fund of reſource, or the moſt habile application of remedy, relieve men under the maladies which ſhe brings upon their affairs. Syſtem alone, as it founds itſelf on the nature of things, and the nature of man, eſtabliſhed in fact and truth, and uniformly purſued with ſpirit, can be adequate to the adminiſtration of the affairs of a State. A Syſtem of this ſpirit and temper in the Rulers will, if there is a ſpirit in the People correſpondent to it, command Fortune. In this ſpirit of ſyſtem, and not in a ſuppoſed predeſtined Fate, did the Fortune of the Roman Republic conſiſt.

<blockquote>Hinc omne Principium, huc refer Exitum.

A line</blockquote>

A line of conduct drawn amidſt the nature of things, and according to the nature of man as connected with them, is, in Politics, what the moral habit of harmonized temper, actuated by uniform Reaſon, is in man. A Syſtem, even the wiſeſt, may, as all human affairs are liable to the effects of external things, be ſtruck by the attacks of Fortune, may not be invulnerable to her ſtrokes; but if it be ſuch as this Memorial ſtates that it ſhould be, "Εργον εἰς ἀιει, and not *in horas*, they will ſtrike it fearleſs; they will ſtrike a breaſt thoroughly prepared to bear up againſt, and finally to repel its effect. Such a Syſtem, in the great and arduous affairs of men, flows through the ever-varying ſeries of Events, like a large and copious river through the varying regions of the earth. Its Greatneſs is not affected by ſmall accidents or incidental chances. The floods of the mountains may pour down in torrents that ſhall diſturb and foul its waters for a ſeaſon, but it holds its courſe, and as it flows, purging

ing off all noxious mixture, clears again to the original purity of its element: the scorching drought of heaven may draw off much of its waters, but the abundance of its original and internal source is superior to such external diminution; and it still holds on its course, in one uniform tenor, equal to all the purposes for which it flows:—it may be precipitated into rapidity in one part of its stream, it may be checked in another; it may be drawn winding through this vale, or forced to make a circuit round that mountain; but its general Course flows uniform to itself, conform to the nature of the country it passes through, and maintains that general direction which its Issue bears to its Source. The conclusion upon the whole is, that, if the New Sovereign Republic of America hath the right conscious sense of *natural liberty and political Freedom*; if it is animated with, and actuated by, *the genuine Spirit of efficient Sovereignty*; if it hath had the wisdom to *harmonize itself within* according to this Spirit, and to form *a grounded and permanent System towards All without*; secured against itself, armed against the Strokes of fortune, and guarded against the malignity of Man; it is established as Nature herself, and will Command: one may not only wish, but as of Nature herself one may pronounce

ESTO PERPETUA.

The Memorial having stated what seemed necessary to the consideration of the Essence, Existence, Efficiency, and assured Permanency of a Republic newly emerging to Independence and established in Sovereignty; it now proceeds to consider matters of Constitution. The Memorialist feels that it would be impertinence towards an American Citizen, and knows that it would be useless and ineffectual to an European Statesman, to enter into the discussion of the particular Constitution of each individual State. The Citizens perfectly know their own Business; and all the force of reason and experience combined will never make the

the

the perverted head of an European, especially a British Statesman, comprehend the Spirit of them. These constitutions are what have wrought the States to Freedom, Independence, and Sovereignty. They are the best that can be at present; and should there be any thing which in future times and circumstances might require a change, there is in these States, as in the animal œconomy, *a healing principle* which will work * itself right.

This Memorial will therefore proceed to consider, in general, as they lie in Nature, *the grounds* on which the General Confederation and Sovereignty stand; and *the principles* by which its Structure and Constitution must take its Form, be that Form whatsoever it may hereafter be.

The principles by which the System of America is animated and actuated, arise from the actual and unconstrained nature

---

* The operation of this is actually provided for in several of the Constitutions of the States, by the establishment of a Census, and other means.

of Things, and from the unperverted, unoppreſſed nature of Man. They are not ſuch Principles as the Political Syſtem of this or that State permits to be called Liberty. The Liberty of the People of America is not merely that ſhare of Power, which an Ariſtocracy permits the People to amuſe themſelves with, and which they are taught to call Liberty. It is not that Domination with which the People govern in a Democracy, and therefore call Liberty. It is not that ſhare of Domination which a political Monarch throws into the hands of the People, in order to ally their power to his Force, by which to govern the Ariſtocracy. The genuine Liberty on which America is founded is totally and intirely a New Syſtem of Things and Men, which treats all as what they actually are, eſteeming nothing the true End and perfect Good of Policy, but that Effect which produces, as equality of Rights, ſo equal Liberty, univerſal Peace, and unobſtructed intercommunion of happineſs in Human Society.

Every

Every Inhabitant of America is, *de facto* as well as *de jure*, equal, in his effential infeparable rights of the individual, to any other Individual; is, in thefe rights, independent of any power that any other can affume over him, over his labour or his property: This is a Principle in act and deed, and not a mere fpeculative Theorem. He is his own mafter both in his reafoning and acting; fo far as refpects the individual, he is at perfect liberty to apply his power as he likes, to labour in any line, and to poffefs and ufe his property as his own. His property is free from any tenure or condition that may clog, obftruct, or divert the fruits of that labour which he hath mixt with it.

There are not in America any Baronial or Manerial Dominations of the leffer but more cruel tyrants. There are not in this Land of Liberty any Feudal, any Perfonal fervices, which may be claimed by a Landlord from the Landholder, whether Prince, Baron, Clergy, or Body Corporate: There are no Fee-farm Rents or Tythes to be paid; there are no deftinations, either of the Refidence or Labour of the Landworker or Mechanic, which in the Old World are affumed as refinements of Polity: neither as a Labourer, nor as a Landworker, does the American ever find himfelf croffed upon by any of thofe felf-obftructive Policies, which have been the bane to Induftry, and blafted the fruits of labour in Europe. He meets nothing which repreffes him back, or excludes him from rifing to that natural importance in the Community, which his ingenuity in his manual labour, or his improvements in his landed Property, muft of courfe, unobftructed, give him. The power which derives from property in America arifes in proportion to the activity which is mixt with it by the poffeffor; and in the hands of thofe who do thus actuate it, it affumes its weight, and relative place, towards the common Center, fo as to render this active Proprietor every day a more important Citizen.

There

There is another Right of the Individual, which the perplext and mixt policy of Europe has broken in upon, and which yet no civil Polity can have cognizance of; and feems to have, as no right, fo no pretence to interfere in: that is, where government affumes a regulating direction over the natural affections of the Sexes. In America, Love and Liberty go hand in hand; and each individual forms thofe connections which nature and the heart point out. Marriage there is a Civil Contract, which is contracted, remains obligatory, or is diffoluble, juft as any other Civil Contract is. This Memorialift knows of * no civil act of State in America which hath ordained any thing to the contrary. The Americans do not as is done in the Mother Country, Firft ftate in their Theology, that *Marriage is*

---

* The Memorial does not enter here into any of thofe ideas which thofe marriages that ufe the forms of the Church of England or of Rome may take up.

no Sacrament, and then continue it in their law and their Police, as *an Act of God,* which no Executive human Power can difannul. Marriage in America is formed directly to anfwer the two great ends for which the two Sexes come together, Private perfonal happinefs, and the propagation of the Species; both which ends are really anfwered in the fulleft and to the moft perfect effect. Every Wife there is herfelf a fortune; and the Children are riches to the parents.

The Right of private confcience in matters of Religion is one of thofe rights which are effential to the individual, and which he cannot alienate or even abate. This is a matter of which Government can have no cognizance, in which it can have no right to interfere: and yet, in the Old World, *this internal* impreffion of the mind of the *Individual,* as though it were *an overt of the Citizen,* hath been treated as an Object in which Government

vernment is supposed to be most deeply interested. On the contrary, the System of the New World considers Religion as an internal act of the Mind towards God, by which Man endeavours to raise up to himself the most perfect notion he can of the Supreme Being, and of his attributes, in order to form his Conduct in moral conformity thereto; also as an act of the mind, by which the internal Man addresses himself in prayer and praise to God, in that way which he thinks most suitable to the Divine Being, and the most efficacious to the obtaining of what he presumes to ask in prayer. This Right therefore exists in America, inviolate, and in perfect liberty.

Another and essential part of the independent political freedom which the American System enjoys is—that it is, as a State, in no wise under the Superintendency of any Ecclesiastical *Imperium* in any shape whatsoever; that it knows no such Solecism as that of the same individual

dual Citizens being the component parts of two diſtinct communities formed under two *diſtinct imperia.*—There is no mixture of any ſuch materials at its foundation; there is no ſuch Frame in any part of its Structure.

The Inhabitants of the Old World, both thoſe who lived under the falſe Religion, as thoſe alſo who dwelt under the manifeſtation of the True, had univerſally their Civil Polity directed in its conſcience by the ſuperintendence and guidance of a Body of Men ſuppoſed to be endued with more than human wiſdom, and who ſeemed to have the power of reward and puniſhment beyond the extent of human power. With the Ancients, before the time of the Manifeſtation of the True Religion, Religion was neither more nor leſs than a State-Engine, framed and worked, under the direction of the Chief Magiſtrate, by the hands and management of the leading Stateſmen, to the purpoſes of the State.

It

It was a Creature of the State. The Christian Religion, a Religion of Spirit and Truth, whose Kingdom was not of this world, whose end and object was in another and future State (for which this life is a preparatory training), was totally abstracted from all Politics, from all Administration and Government of the things of this world; and had no other concern therein, but to render unto Cæsar those things which are Cæsar's, and to be obedient to the higher Powers: yet so it hath happened (I suppose the divine Teachers of this religion found it necessary), that, when they established their System, as an outward visible form, they formed an intermediate temporal Community and *Imperium*, both ecclesiastical and civil, in and over the things and Persons of this world: and, feeling themselves as an independent distinct Body politic, assumed *either an ascendant superintendence over the Civil Community*, or put themselves in the predicament

cament of having formed, on original compact, *an alliance between the Church and the State.* The State of Europe (it may be said, of the whole Roman Empire) at the firſt origin of Civil Governments under the Conquerors of that Empire, was ſuch as naturally gave birth and ſcope to this Syſtem. The commanding paramount powers of the Great, and the ſeveral *imperia* of the leſſer Commanders, who had overran and held in Subjection all Europe, were merely Military. The idea of Government, other than that of military diſcipline within their Camps, Cantonments, and the Poſts of their reſpective armies, entered not into their Syſtem. Theſe People had no idea of civil government as neceſſary to be co-extenſive with the predominant military *Imperium.* They conſidered all civil polity as mere matter of œconomy in a family, clan, or horde; as mere ſubordinate arrangement of the community of any people or nation; which the body could beſt ſettle for itſelf,

and

and be beft anfwerable for. Of what form this was, or how adminiftered, was matter of indifference to thefe Commanders. This civil line and field, therefore, was opened to all Inftitutors of Politics, who could acquire afcendency fufficient to eftablifh themfelves under the aufpices of the military.

At this period the Human Species in Europe, howfoever trained and difciplined to, howfoever exercifed and expert in war, could, as to political civilization, fcarce be faid to have emerged out of their Savage State. The Miffionaries of Rome were fent out amongft thefe, to teach them the arts of focial life, to civilife them, and to convert them to the Chriftian Religion. Thefe Miffionaries (I mean fome of the firft) had defervedly great merit with them, and acquired thereby an almoft abfolute afcendency over them: they became their Farmers, Mechanics, Artifts, their lawyers, their judges, their Lawgivers, their guides, and the directors of their opinions and confciences. Whatever Polities,

Polities, therefore, grew up amidst these thus first civilized Europeans, were interwoven at the root, and grew up interbranching with ecclesiastical Government, so as not to be separable from it. The lands and property of the ecclesiastical society (however obtained) came forward into improvement and fixed property, co-eval (if not in a leading line) with the property of the Civil Body, and, as it were, allied and intermixed with it. In the European States, therefore, the Ecclesiastical Rights, Property, Polity, and *Imperium*, became, from the earliest periods of Civilization, an essential, inseparable part of the Constitution. Whatever may be the abstract truth in civil Polity, taken *à priori* in its original principles; whatever may be the opinion of men in these days; the fact and invariable precedent is, that in Europe the ecclesiastical *Imperium* or * Church is an indefeasible part of the

---

* " The Clergy of England have a Zeal for the
" Church of England; but they have a greater Zeal
" for

the State. And every loyal subject of these States will be, at least ought to be, a zealous maintainer of this United or allied establishment of Church and State.

It is not so with the Americans, and the system of America. They were not thus civilized by ecclesiastical Missionaries. No Church power was their foster Parent. The Original Constituents of these States were in a perfect state of Civilization, in perfect independence and freedom, at the establishment of their Civil Polity. An ecclesiastical Body, as a separate Community from the Civil Community, and yet formed of the same individuals, would have appeared to them as a Chimera. The System in which American Polity is built up stands independent, and is free from those heterogeneous mix-

---

"for the Church of Christ: there are Few of them, I hope, who scruple professing a Wish, that the pure banner of the Gospel may, if need shall so require, be displayed triumphant on the ruins of every Church Establishment in Christendom."
—A Letter from the Lord Bishop of Landaff, to his Grace the Archbishop of Canterbury, p. 3.

tures, which always more or less * obstructed each other, and which drew into crookedness and obliquities the free and natural Energy of Both. The Americans have no one Form of ecclesiastical system, or Church established as *the Religion of the State*; they have *no landed clergy*; no Church Revenue derived by a transfer of the slavish Tax of Tythes from the State to the Church: their lands were never *Agri Decumanni*. They do not apply Religion, as was the case in the false religion, as an engine of State; but considering it *as what it is*, they make the proper distinction which its divine Author made: they give unto God the things which are God's; and unto Cæsar [*i. e.* the Civil State] the things which are Cæsar's. In this they have no part to take, but to

---

* The purity of Religion equally suffered by this worldly alliance of the Daughter of God with the Child and Creature of Man; as Civil Government hath done by the Constraints with which this high-spirited Dame on earth hath bound the energy of its Freedom.

follow

follow God and Nature in the direct right line of Truth.

The System of the American Community lies in Nature: from natural causes there is now, has been, and most likely will continue to be, a general equality, not only in the Persons, but in the power of the landed Property of the Inhabitants. This Basis of the superstructure is uniform and level; the *Res Populi*, the *actuated Rights and Interests* of the People, is every where equally attended to, and is in all points coming forward (if I may so express myself) in parallel lines into operation. This equal level of acting powers and actuated property, lying thus in Nature, becomes, by the vigour of natural principles, the Basis of a Free Republic. This is the grand *Desideratum* of all the ancient Legislators and Institutors of Republics. They saw the necessity that there was of an exact conformity between the Constitution of the State, and the *Species of Individuals*, the *form of the community*, and *nature of the basis* on which such State must be founded. No such Basis was there found in nature; they therefore tried a thousand different projects to form such in Art. They forced Nature. Not finding the natural situation of men to be what it was necessary to the System of their Polity it should be, they endeavoured to make it what it never could be, but under force and violence done to nature. They destroyed or perverted all Personal Liberty, in order to force into establishment Political Freedom. While Men were taught by pride, and by a prospect of Domination over others, to call The State Free, they found themselves cut off from, and from the use of, many of the essential inalienable rights of the Individual, which form his happiness as well as freedom. So far from finding themselves free, they felt themselves mere machines. All this was done and suffered, to obtain (which yet they never could obtain) that natural equal level Basis on which Ye, American

can Citizens, stand; on which Ye, United States of America, are built up, in a manner that combines the perfect possession of the rights of the Individual, Personal liberty, and Political Freedom.

Here, UNITED STATES AND CITIZENS OF AMERICA! look back on the peculiar blessings, on the special favours, on the singular happiness, in which Providence hath been pleased to establish your System; to which he hath seemed to select you, as a chosen people, in a New World, separate and removed far from the regions and wretched Politics of the Old one. Consider this well, not only in the conscious feel of the happiness which you yourselves enjoy, and which it is your Duty to deliver unabated over to your Children; but in the sincere sense of gratitude which Heaven demands of you. Manifest this in the conduct and Administration of your Sovereign Powers, while you establish, as constitutional maxims in practice, those Truths which

form

form the principles of your Syſtem.— *Serendi Sunt Mores.*—I do not here mean a new cultivation: for the Manners and Spirit of the Americans have been, uniformly, what juſt ſuch a ſtate, ſuch a Syſtem of Things would inſpire; and their political Character, juſt that habit of Conduct which is conform to it: a character, which looks to rights of perfect freedom as the firſt object and end of man as a Citizen; that eſtimates all men as equals; and is no reſpecter of perſons, but according to their place in thoſe orders and ſubordinations which the State gives, and which therefore reſpects the office, not the man: a character that knows how to eſtimate the Majeſty of the People, and the *Imperium* of the State; and honours and obeys it for real conſcience ſake: a character by which each individual conſiders himſelf as a * Participant with his fellow Citizens, and a Commu-

---

* Ad participandum alium ab alio, communicandumq; inter omnes. *Cicero* de Leg. Lib. i. § 11.

nicant

nicant in the Whole; and therefore feels, as a felf-confcious feel, an unaffected, inartificial, natural Love for his Country, combined with a prompt and ardent zeal for its Service. It is this fpirit and this Character, which hath wrought You up to the independent Free Sovereigns which you now are. When, therefore, this Memorial prefumes to advance this propofition, *Serendi funt Mores*, it means that the fame Culture of *Political Character* be regularly continued; that the fame Senfe of Your Syftem, the Same Spirit of Liberty, the fame manners may remain unabated, unaltered, undepraved, to form and animate the fame Character; for on Cuftoms and manners, more than on Laws and Imperium, depends the fate, the fortune, and the exiftence of a State. And may this, many ages yet to come, not only be faid of You, but be true, which Ennius faid of Rome:

* Moribus antiquis Res ftat Romana, Virifq;

* It is impoffible that the import of the truth and wifdom of this propofition can be too ftrongly
impreffed

That, thus founded in Nature, and thus built up in Truth, Your States should arise to Independence and Sovereignty in the very spirit of Political Freedom; that, under a system so entirely new upon

_{impressed on the mind of a free Citizen of America; and lest the quotation of it above should not make a sufficient impression, I cannot but here insert—Cicero's Commentary on it.—Quem quidem Ille [Ennius] versum, vel brevitate vel veritate, tanquam ex oraculo mihi quodam esse effatus videtur. Nam neq; Viri, nisi ita morata Civitas fuisset, neq; Mores, nisi hi Viri præfuissent, aut fundare, aut tam diù tenere potuissent tantam, & tam longè latèq imperantem Rempub. Itaq; ante nostram memoriam, & mos ipse patrius præstantes Viros adhibebat, & veterem morem ac majorum instituta retinebant excellentes Viri. Nostra verò ætas cum rempublicam sicut picturam accipisset egregiam, sed jam evanescentem vetustate, non modo eam coloribus iisdem, quibus fuerat, renovare neglexit, sed ne id quidem curavit, ut formam saltem ejus, & extrema tanquam lineamenta servaret. Quid enim manet ex antiquis moribus, quibus ille dixit Rem stare Romanam? Quos ita oblivione obsoletos videmus, ut non modo non colantur, sed etiam ignorantur. Num de Viris quid dicam? Mores enim ipsi interierunt Virorum penuriâ. Cujus tanti Mali non modo reddenda Ratio nobis, sed etiam tanquam Reis capitis quodammodo dicenda causa est. Nostris enim Vitiis, non casu aliquo, Rempublicam verbis retinemus, reapsa vero jampridem amisimus. *Ciceronis de Repub.* Lib. v. Fragm.}

Earth,

Earth, your improvement should continually so expand; that your population should so increase and multiply; that a Civilizing activity, beyond what Europe could ever know, should animate and actuate your progression; that your commercial and Naval power should be found active in almost every quarter of the Globe; that your Military power should be equal to the defence, and your political wisdom adequate to the establishment of your Sovereignty, is and was but a natural Consequence in the ordinary train of Causes and Effects. It was due and just to you thus to state You to the Sovereigns of Europe; and there was no advice so good could be given to them, as *the Stating of this simple Fact*, so little understood in the Old World. The Memorial addressed to these Sovereigns stated it without reserve or disguise. This truth was at first treated as unintelligible speculation. It was unfashionable; it was neglected where it was not rejected, but in general it was rejected as inadmissible: by degrees it entered into the reasoning of many an individual; and when it was in various translations expanded in Europe, it was found insensibly to have mixed itself with the sentiments of many a Statesman, and at length reached the ear and penetrated the heart of some Sovereigns---lastly, those of the Ministers and Sovereign of Great-Britain. This truth, which had been for some years considered as a Proposition not to be listened to, not to be suffered to be mentioned; for the enouncing of which (although * in the line of his duty) the Author was called, by the Wise Men of the British Cabinet, *a Wild Man*, unfit to be employed; yet this Truth became, in about a year and a half, demonstration not to be resisted, and an universal idea of Europe. *Magna est vis veritatis, & prævaluit.* Great-Britain reaped the fruits of the wisdom of its ministers; and Truth and Right were established in peace.

* In his Speeches in Parliament, on December 2, 1777, and March 17, 1783, wherein he recommended the making a Fœderal Treaty with America.

This

This Memorial will now proceed to state the System of America so far as relates to the formation and constitution of the General Government of the Confederated Sovereignty of America. * " Neque
" prorsus diffidere debeo, quin' possim de
" hac re fortasse, non imperitè nec in-
" utiliter differere; utpote qui longa †
" experientiâ edoctus, & per tot munerum
                                                       " &

---

* *Bacon* de augmentis Scientiarum. Lib. iii. Cap. 8.

† Especially in this point of Policy, the grounds and reasons, the ways and means, of Union and Confederation between States, such as the Free ones of America.

This Memorialist was at the Congress at Albany in 1754, and cognizant both of the measures and the reasons of the measures adopted there.

He, as a Commissioner from the Province, now the State Massachusett's-bay, in 1755, negotiated with New-York, New-Jersey, and Pennsylvania, the Confederated expedition, in union with New England, against Crown Point; and Succeeded.

And, lastly, when he was Governor of Massachusett's-bay, he formed, in 1758, a Plan of an Union of the Provinces, Colonies, and Plantations, of New-England, for their mutual Protection and Defence against the Common Enemy, which was actually concerted and settled by Commissioners from Massachusett's-bay, and the Commissioners of the Colony of Connecticut, convened at Boston:

"& honorum gradus ad ampliſſimum
"[Coloniarum] Magiſtratum evectus fu‑
"erim, eundemq; magiſtratum per annos
"quoſdam geſſerim."

The Memorial hath explained in what manner and by what principles the Syſtem of America ſtands on the natural baſis of a Republic. The deſcribing how it is built up in its *Frame* in conformity to this foundation, is coming to the point of *Conſtitution*.

The People at large in the multitude are in a natural incapacity of exerciſing their Reaſoning powers; and very inconveniently ſituated and circumſtanced to give by every Individual their Judgment and Reſult. There is no regular way of collecting the wiſdom and ſenſe of the People as a Community, but by ſome delegated repreſentation, to ſuch numbers as may be in a capacity of Reaſoning and

---

to which the Province New-Hampſhire, the Colony Rhode-Iſland, and Providence Plantation, were invited to accede.——The change of Men and Meaſure in the Military Command in America which took place that year, rendered this meaſure unneceſſary, and it was laid aſide.

Debate;

Debate; * and no means (some cases excepted) of collecting the sense of the whole, but by delegation of power to a part to give the dissent or consent for the whole. If the People, as in America, are in the full and perfect use and enjoyment of their equal Liberty, they will, as in the ordinary process of their operations, form their own actual Representation; they will naturally find out where the wisdom of the Community lies, and will delegate their power of reason and debate to that part. They will find out almost mechanically to whom and in what manner they may delegate the power of giving their Dissent or Consent, and of converting the Wisdom of the State into the Law of the Land.

This is the *Actual* State of America. The universal sense of the People is collected, and operates in Debate and Result on the universal interest of the People.

* A Popular Assembly, rightly ordered, brings up every one in his turn to give the Result of the whole People. *Harrington's* System of Politics. Chap. v. 24.

This

This is the existence by nature, and in fact of a republic, *Respublica est Res Populi*. Populus autem non omnis Cœtus multitudinis, sed Cœtus juris consensu, & utilitatis communione sociatus.

Exactly as the several separate States are formed on this System and by these principles, so is the general Confederation by the establishment and Constitution of its Government. The Reason of the whole is delegated to, and the Wisdom of the whole is concentered in, the Congress. And this Institution arises from those principles, and by those operations, which actuate a Free Republic: The Liberty of the People, manifested by the sense of the whole, coincides, co-operates, and exists in it. Neither the opinions of assuming Leaders, nor the intrigues of caballing Factions, will be found there, or at least will not survive a moment. The Sense of the whole is what must predominate, actuate, and govern throughout, in all opinions, in all measures of effect and permanency. In Great Britain, where the

Members of Parliament do not come together as representing *the Sense and reasoning of the People* at large; they must have some time to form *their own* opinion. A certain leading Judgment *does this for them*; and as often as this leading judgment changes *its* opinion, these Members, or a majority of them, will be found to have changed *their* opinion in all extreams of contraries. This instability hath, and will ever attend them, although members of a permanent Body; while the Congress, an annual institution, consisting of many new Members at every re-election, hath in its opinions, its resolutions and measures, manifested a degree of united firmness, a continued uniformity in opinion, and unalterable perseverance in a System of wise and effective measures. The true and real reason of this is, that this System was the decided, determined opinion of the Body of the People, whom those Members of Congress *really represented*. Experience has confirmed what Wisdom saw before, that there

there could not be a measure more surely grounded than this Institution by which the Confederation acts in Congress. If it be viewed arising from the actual State of things and Men, and by the natural energy thereof, it will be seen that there could not be a measure more judiciously, more politically constituted, to actuate the reason, to collect the Wisdom of the Union, and to bring it forward into action. There cannot be a stronger proof of the Temper, Prudence, and assured confidence, which the People have in the foundation of their Liberties, than the entrusting in delegation the great and extensive Powers with which they have invested Congress; nor can there be in any Rulers a greater Merit with the People, than the Spirited yet cautious, the Liberal yet guarded Use that these Members of Congress have made of them.

The ordinary mode of administration into which General Councils distribute themselves, is, by the Members dividing themselves in several Chambers or
Boards,

Boards, according to the several branches of business to be done, and erecting these into separate Offices. The Deputies of the States of the Belgic United Provinces formed themselves into three Councils; the Council called the States-General, the Council of State, and the Chamber of Accounts. The Command of the Army and Navy, which might have divided them into two more departments, were vested in the Counts or Stadtholder of each Province, as Captain General and Admiral. These Offices always have either too little or too much power, and are, in the one extreme, inefficient to the purpose of administrative power; or, in the other, form dangerous precedents against the equal balance of power in the Constitution of a Republic; or create distraction, opposition, and interfering obstruction, in the Commissions and other delegated powers which act under each department. The Administration of the business of the Government of Great-Britain by such Boards, gives daily proof of this. The Prudence, Experience, and Wisdom of Congress,

Congress, have avoided the forming of any such Offices, Boards, or Chambers: They from time to time appoint such Commitees, with such powers, as the emergent case may require; or such standing Committees as a permanent course of Affairs in any one line may render necessary; which Committees, while they continue, may apply to Congress from time to time for such further powers as may become necessary. This application will give Congress a proper opportunity of revising the business, and of considering, whether they will grant further powers, or whether the business doth not become of such importance as that they should take it into their own cognizance and management. This is a much wiser mode of casting the business of an Administration of a Republic. It is, indeed, a line of conduct that is peculiar to, and distinguishes the wisdom of, Congress.

The Memorialist takes now the liberty which, as a Citizen of the World, he feels he hath in him, that of giving his opinion

even

even where he presumes to doubt upon any measure of Congress. By the fifth section of the eighth Article of the Confederation, "the States assembled in Con-
"gress shall have authority to appoint a
"Committee of the States *to sit in the re-*
"*cess of Congress.*" Experience is derived from comparing one measure and its consequences with another, that being similar may have similar consequences. "The
"States General" (saith Sir William Temple, in his Treatise on the Constitution of the Belgic Union) "used to be convoked
"by the Council of State; but the Pro-
"vinces and their Delegates, growing
"jealous of that power, perhaps from a
"misuser of it, formed an *Ordinary Council*
"*called the States General,* which is *only*
"*a representation* of the States General,
"though always called by that name. The
"*Real Whole Body* of the States General
"*never sits;* this so called sits continually."
Compare this Case to that of the *Committee of States sitting in the Recess of Congress.* Does it not seem, from this example, if rightly understood and rightly applied,

applied, that some caution is necessary, lest *the Committee of the States sitting in the recess* of Congress, the representative of a representation, should *in ordinary* supersede Congress? And does not the occasion of appointing such a Committee arise from a defect, namely, that of providing for the Administrative part of Government?

The observation, which the Memorial is led next to make, requires much apology; and is made with all deference to the wisdom of Congress; and the Memorialist confides in the candour of the Sovereigns of America, that they will not be offended, if he assumes in this point no more liberty than he did in his address to the Sovereigns of Europe. The Memorialist, persuaded of the truth of his opinion on the matter, as he conceives it to lie, and yet differing so directly from a decided opinion and measure of Congress, fears that he does not rightly or perfectly understand the case. Collecting, however, his ideas from the Act of Confederation, he cannot but think, that sufficient and adequate provision is not made for the

Repre-

Reprefenting of the MAJESTY OF THE PEOPLE, THE SOVEREIGNTY OF THE UNITED STATES; nor for the efficient Adminiftration of the intereft and powers of the Confederation as a General Government. From fome lingering doubt of themfelves, from fome excefs of diftruft in men, from fome defect in that affured confidence, which a People, founded in political freedom, and built up to Sovereignty, ought to have in their Syftem, they feem (at leaft fo it appears to the Memorialift) to have been afraid to eftablifh a Supreme Magiftracy, to give effect to, and to carry into execution, in a continued courfe of Adminiftration, the refolves, orders, and meafures of Congrefs. And yet their whole fyftem, the forms of bufinefs, the procedure of the operations of the refpective States, and the circumftances in which the American people at large found themfelves at the time of the late Revolution, led as naturally to fome fuch eftablifhment; as the Syftem and Circumftances of the Roman People, when

when they drove out their King, and abolished perſonal Domination, led to the eſtabliſhing of the Adminiſtrative, Executive Magiſtracy in annual Conſuls.

Previous to the reaſoning in which the Memorial now proceeds to recommend the mixture of *Monarchical forms* of office in the Adminiſtrative branch of Magiſtracy, it may be proper to avow and declare the Memorialiſt's opinion of Government by a Monarch, claiming any perſonal right of *Imperium* over the State and People as his Dominion in property; it is a proper caution; that he may not be miſtaken, or even ſuſpected, when his ideas and words go only to that monarchical Magiſtrate, who merely as an official temporary reſponſible Officer adminiſters, in rotation, the *Res Populi*, the Commonwealth; as though he had a drift, by a ſuppoſitious meaſure, to lay the ground for the Reſtoration of Monarchy. The Words of Mr. Harrington will beſt expreſs it: " I could never be perſuaded, " but that it was more happy for a people " to be diſpoſed of by a number of perſon

"sons jointly interested and concerned
" with them, than to be numbered as the
" Herd and inheritance of One, to whose
" lust and madness they were absolutely
" subject: and that any Man, even of the
" weakest reason and generosity, would
" not rather chuse for his habitation that
" Spot of Earth, where there was access
" to Honour by Virtue, and where no
" Worth could be excluded, rather than
" that where all advancement should pro-
" ceed from the Will of one scarcely hear-
" ing and seeing with his own organs,
" and gained for the most part by means
" lewd and indirect; and all this in the
" end to amount to nothing else than a
" more splendid and dangerous slavery."
Although this be the opinion of the Memorialist, the Memorial will not presume to proceed in its opinions, but under the reasoning of that genuine Patriot, and decided Republican, BRUTUS, as contained in the advice which he gave to the Roman People at the Crisis of their revolution from Monarchy to a Commonwealth.

" The

"The first essential business" * (saith this Great Man) "is to set ourselves quite clear and rid of the Monarch, so as to leave no doubts, no hopes, so as to risque no danger of our falling back to that System of Tyranny in personal domination. This step secured; we shall at our ease and leisure be Free to make such alterations and correction in the Office, as may be found safest and best for the future administration of our Republic; by a Magistracy of a different institution, executing the necessary powers of this Branch of Government, altered, corrected, limited, controuled, and responsible at the Expiration of their temporary *Imperium*. The evils which were derived upon us from the Monarch, as holding and exercising his power *as of personal right*, must be immediately and radically taken away and removed; and the office must be guarded against all

---

* *Dionys. Halycarn.* Lib. iv.

"possibility of relapse into Tyranny for the future. The Office itself should be abridged in its duration, and limited in its powers, in all reference to personal prerogative; in every circumstance and thing which may give the most distant occasion to *continued or Personal* Government. The Officer or Officers, who shall be thought the proper ones to administer this Office, should not retain, even in idea or name, the least trace of Government residing in their persons, but in the Office: and that they are *only the Administrators of a Government directed by the Senate*, and that they *act by the advice thereof*, and *under the authority of the same*. The Magistrate or Magistrates should be elected, and that *only for a year*, in successive rotation of Persons. He then declares his decided Opinion, that it should not be entrusted to, nor be permitted to be executed by One Person, but by Two, having equal concurrent Powers and Jurisdiction.

" The Government, thus bipartite, will
" be a check upon itself; and each Offi-
" cer muſt act cautiouſly with reference
" to his Colleague. There will, by this
" diviſion of the Magiſtracy, be created
" an emulation for the obtaining the good
" opinion of the People, if not in both,
" in one at leaſt, in proportion as the
" other by his conduct is loſing it.
" Laſtly, and above all, the delegated
" Power which is committed to the
" Officer or Officers who are to adminiſ-
" ter and execute this Office, ſhould be
" limited in time. As there is nothing ſo
" ſtrongly prompts, teaches, and tempts a
" Man to annex power to himſelf perſo-
" nally, and to enterpriſe the extent of it;
" nothing which renders the Attempt ſo
" ſafe, and perhaps at length ſo neceſ-
" ſary, as diſtant and incertain reſponſi-
" bility, as the being unlimited in the
" duration of the time for which he
" holds his power : So, on the other
" hand, nothing ſo truly and effectually
" forms the republican character of the
" Officer

" Officer chosen to govern, as that he
" should in his person, and in turn of ro-
" tation, obey as well as command; that
" his delegated powers should expire as
" soon, and at as short a period, as is con-
" sistent with efficient Government; and
" that, at the end of his administration,
" he should as of course be responsible,
" and answer to the People for it. These
" matters thus constituted and establish-
" ed, you will not only be guarded against
" all personal Domination, against the
" evils arising or deriving from a Mo-
" narch; but you may, on the other hand,
" freely use, exercise, and enjoy, all those
" advantages arising from the prompt,
" efficient, and continued administration
" of the Executive Branch through *Mo-*
" *narchical* forms, combined with the
" Aristocratic and the Controul of the
" Popular Branches in the same Com-
" monwealth. Considering these mat-
" ters, and that the forms of your pro-
" ceedings in business have been of this
" sort, I should doubt whether your pru-
" dence

" dence would at prefent make any fur-
" ther alteration in your Conftitution *."

To this the Memorial adjoins the coinciding opinion of one of the trueft Patriots and firft Republican Statefmen of the World of bufinefs. † Cicero fays, *Refpublica eft Res Populi---Statuo effe optimè conftitutam Rempublicam quæ ex tribus generibus illis, Regali, Optimo, & Populari, confufa eft modicè.* Alfo the opinion of a decided Englifh Republican, *Mr. Harrington*---" A Commonwealth confifts of
" a Senate propofing, a people refolving,
" and the *magiftracy executing*; whereby
" partaking of the Ariftocracy in the Se-
" nate, of the Democracy in the People,

---

* The Memorial here gives, in a free tranflation, the Sum and purport, rather than the clofe tenor, of this Speech; rather than copying the manner, it gives the fpirit of this wife counfel of Brutus, on which the Roman Republic, at its firft great revolution was eftablifhed. The Editor did think of putting the Speech itfelf in the original, in the margin; but, on fecond thoughts, decided that it was mere trifling to fill two or three pages with Greek to no purpofe. The learned reader, if he feels himfelf interefted, will refer to it.

† Fragment. *Ciceronis* de Repub. Lib. ii.

" and

" and of Monarchy in the Magiftracy, it
" is complete. Now, there being no other
" Commonwealth but this in Art or Na-
" ture, it is no wonder that the Ancients
" held this only to be good."

After thefe authorities, the Memorialift prefumes to offer, with all humility and deference, his own reafoning, applied to the prefent State of the American Confederation. It feems to this Memorialift, that, to infure to itfelf efficiency and permanency; to affure all other Powers, which can have any negotiation or alliances with it, of its having full powers and authorities, not only to treat and to conclude, but to carry into actual effect whatever it binds itfelf to in Treaty; the general Confederation, the general Government, wants fomething to infure in all cafes the *Confenfus Obedientium* of all the States, to thofe meafures, the carrying of which into execution depends on the diftinct Sovereignty of each State. The Congrefs met at Albany, felt the fame difficulty, and found that in practice

tice this fame defect might occur. What they as Commiffioners of fubordinate dependent Provinces adopted, might fuit them as fubject to a Superior paramount Government, but can by no means be even talked of in the cafe of independent Sovereigns. In confequence, however, of the Independence and Sovereignty of each State, fome thing hath appeared as wanting. What that fomething fhould be, the Memorialift does not prefume, even in his own mind, to form an idea of, much lefs to write or fpeak of. If, on any occafion, the Delegates of any particular State, being in a Minority on any Queftion, the State who fent thofe Delegates fhould think, that Congrefs had exceeded the Powers with which it is invefted, or had miftaken and not acted conform to them, and fhould therefore withhold the *confenfus obedientium*; Political logic will never be wanting to give fcope to fuch evil. If there are no fuch Symptoms through which Congrefs meets with difficulties; if what this Memorialift hath

been

been led to fear, and through excefs of anxiety hath prefumed to mention as an Object of fear, is unfounded, he begs pardon, and confides alone in the Spirit of liberality, which animates Congrefs, for forgivenefs. If any fuch Symptoms have, however latent, been felt; the caution, although it may be, as Demofthenes faid to the Citizens of Athens, neither prudent nor pertinent in me to mention, is, neverthelefs, *always neceffary for You*, UNITED STATES AND CITIZENS, *to take to your bofoms.*

The Articles of Confederation mark, that there are many Matters refpecting the general Intereft of the States, and their Bufinefs, which muft be referred to Congrefs: the Deliberation, the deciding opinions and Refolutions upon thofe matters, and the originating of Meafures to be taken thereupon, muft certainly be trufted to Congrefs, and cannot any where elfe be fo truly and fafely trufted. Congrefs, however, feems to be formed on the Idea of a Senate to debate, or of a

Council

Council to advife; and there feems to be (at leaft it fo feems to this Memorialift) *a neceffity of a diftinct Branch of Magiftracy for Adminiftration:* an office executed by fome officer or officers that fhall be refponfible to the States at large. If the fame Body whofe Refult forms *the Reafon of State*, and hath full power and authority to decide and refolve what is *right to be done* in the General Government, is to adminifter this reafon of State, and to execute the meafure decided on; there can be no refponfibility: and fhould even, in future depravations of men, fuch cafes arrive, that a Majority of fome future Congrefs fhould be devoted to the fentiments of fome foreign Court, THE UNITED STATES may be injured within the year of that Congrefs, without remedy: whereas, were two Confuls (Protectors, Stadtholders, Prefidents, or officers by any other Title) annually elected, who fhould adminifter and execute (under the Authority and by the advice of Congrefs) the General Bufinefs of the

UNITED

United States, and limited in their power thus only to act, so as that any Act, not thus authorised and advised, should be null and void respecting the States, and Criminal respecting the Acting Magistrates; the Confederation could not be betrayed. And if, in order to manifest the Authority and Legality of these Executing Administering Officers, it should be a necessary accompaniment, that every Act should be countersigned by the Secretary of Congress; no Persons or States whom it might concern could be deceived. These Magistrates, to prevent any collusion between them and a corrupt majority of Congress, ought to be held responsible to the States at large, for executing any measures, even though advised by Congress, if such measures were fundamentally contrary to the Constitution, or directly injurious *Rei Populi*, or did in any mode betray the interest of the States to foreign powers: and at the same time these Magistrates, that in fair justice they might be able to act clear of blame under this Rcfponfibility, ought to have a power, if they faw Caufe, jointly or feparately, of fufpending their Acting, until they could refer the matter of Doubt to the Several States refpectively. "As "the *hand* of the Magiftrate would be, "by this Inftitution, the Adminiftrator of "*the Reafon* of State and the Execu- "tor of the Law; fo the *head* of that "Magiftrate ought to be anfwerable to "the People that his conduct is directed "by that reafon of State, and his execu- "tion conform to that Law *." Such a Magiftrate will be in a natural incapacity of doing wrong himfelf, and will be from prudence and Self-fafety an efficient check over any very dangerous errors or mif- chievous Intrigues of Congrefs. The Memorialift does not here prefume to Speak of the Extent or Limitation of the Powers which fhould be vefted in fuch Magiftrates; he will only fay, as an un- controvertible truth, that they fhould be fuch as are efficient to Adminiftration and Execution.

* Mr. Harrington.

Execution. If they are not, the Inſtitution is a Mockery: and if the United States and Citizens of America heſitate to delegate ſuch to an annual elective ſucceſſion of Magiſtrates in rotation, they have not within themſelves a real grounded aſſurance in the foundation of their own Syſtem; they are not perfectly confirmed and ſatisfied in the conſciouſneſs of their Political Freedom.

The Wiſdom and Authority of the Congreſs is the concentration of the reaſon and powers of the ſeveral States; as is, in like manner, each State the concentration of the reaſon and powers of its reſpective Citizens. The Sovereignty and *Imperium* of the Magiſtracy in each State, is the concentring Repreſentative of the Majeſty of the People of that State. There ſeems (at leaſt to the apprehenſion of this Memorialiſt) to be wanting, in the General Government of the Confederation, a like concentred Repreſentative of the Majeſty of the People at large, and of the General Sovereignty of the United States.

As Man confifts of Body as well as mind; fo, in all matters with which his political exiftence is connected, there muft be an actual office externally and materially exifting, as *the refidence of Majefty and Sovereignty in perfonal Exiftence*, with which the Majefty and Sovereignty of other States may treat and act.

If, according to experience derived from the Wifdom and Fortune of Rome, THE UNITED STATES fhould be of opinion to inftitute fuch an office, the refidence of Majefty and Sovereignty; and to Create two equal Magiftrates with concurrent jurifdiction, as above defcribed, to adminifter and execute thefe concentred Powers; they will, as that State did, cloath this officer or officers with all the enfigns of Majefty, and all the outward marks of Executive power; with all the honours and dignities that fhould attend and adorn the actual Reprefentative presentative of the Majesty of the People; so that its authority may be seen and felt, as well as its powers obeyed, within the General Government. They will so hold out the staff, and set up on high the Standard of their Sovereignty to all Nations, that its equal State may stand acknowledged, that its *Fecial* rights, its war establishment, the Rank of its Staff, and of its Officers, may be, by decided acknowledgment of Nations, known and avowed; that the Respect due to its flag, the Authority of its Passes, Letters of Mark, and the Rank of its Fleets and Seamen, may be settled as of common and reciprocal right; that the *several orders of Citizens*, in this New Republican State, may have, in perfect reciprocity, relative place and precedence amongst the *respective orders of subjects* in the several States of Europe; that its Commerce may, in its operations and interests, enjoy full and perfect liberty, such as it gives.

All the Forms of Office, all proceedings in business, all the modes of Administration,

niſtration, all the acts of Government in the reſpective States, when they were Provinces and Colonies, were Monarchical. Moſt of the States have preſerved the ſame Forms in their reſpective New-eſtabliſhed Sovereign Conſtitutions; nor are they leſs Commonwealths or Republics for taking this mixed form; but, as hath been ſaid above, ſo much the more firmly founded in Cuſtoms, Nature, and Truth. How, then, will the General Government be the leſs a Republic for taking the like form, or why leſs to be truſted with it? May the Memorialiſt, therefore, venture to ſay, UNITED STATES AND CITIZENS of America, conſider and treat yourſelves *as what you are*; and act upon your Syſtem *as being what it is:* and know *that it is* that beſt of all conſtituted Republics, that, in which the Monarchical, Ariſtocratic, and Popular Forms, are all combined in concert with each other.

If any doubts, fears, or jealouſies, of the reſtoration of the Monarch, agitate the minds

minds of the States and Citizens; the appointment of this new-reformed office, framed and interwoven into the Constitution of the Commonwealth, with powers that efficiently and to all purposes fulfil and execute all the duties of the Monarch, will, as it did at Rome, effectually for ever stifle every thought and wish that could look to such Restoration, and exclude all possibility of any such event taking place. Had the people of England, after the death of Charles the First, and the exile of the rest of the Royal Family, been in a capacity of taking up the precedent of Rome, and appointed an annual Magistracy---a Protector---or two Consuls, to execute the office of Protector or King, there never would have been a Restoration. But the Nation, finding no regular, constitutional, Administrative Power; but, instead thereof, feeling the arbitrary power of every ascendant Faction, did, under one common sympathy, and unanimously, (if that expression can be said of an act where no concert or
common

common consent was taken,) revolt from the Government in Possession, and recoil back into Monarchy; and to the Monarch.

The only thing which can ever, in America, create a danger of falling back to the imagination or desire of a Monarch, will be the leaving of the General Government defective, *sinè Magistratu & Imperio* in the Executive Administrative Branch. If there be not a fixed permanent office, that may be the center of information; the Repertory and Record of the concentred wisdom of the People, of the Reason of State; that may be the constant, uniform, never-ceasing spring of action in the administration and management of the general Interest, the general government of the UNITED STATES; this Government must at times be at a stand, its powers suspended, and always liable to be inefficient. This *desideratum* will lead uneasy, unsettled, restless minds, to other *desiderata*; and if this chain of reasoning, or of adopting opinions, once takes

takes place with a people, who shall say to what it may or may not train? More is to be apprehended from the deficiency of this Branch of Government, than it is possible should derive from any establishment of such a Magistracy, and such annual responsible Magistrates, as this Memorial presumes to recommend. The Constitution of Rome was ruined by the advantages taken in various measures from the want of a proper elective Assembly, representative of the People; and the creation of an † unlimited Magistrate, to actuate their factions. If any thing could have saved this Constitution, the Office of Consul would have saved it.

All that is here said, refers to the Establishment of the Empire, *as to Peace and Polity*: the Congress, with a General and Commander in Chief of the Army, was sufficient for *War*—* *Sed in posterum firmanda Respublica, non armis modo, neq; adversum Hostes, sed, quod multò majus, multòq; asperius est, bonis Pacis artibus.*

The Memorial here closes what it hath

† The Tribune.   * Salluft ad Cæfarem.

P

presumed to advance upon the matter of Constitution; and quoting an opinion of Mr. Hume, namely, " That Legislators " ought not to trust the future Govern- " ment of a State to Chance, but ought " to provide a System of Laws to regu- " late the Administration of public af- " fairs to the latest Posterity," will hope that what it hath recommended will make a serious impression on the minds of the Americans in the true sense of this wise and interesting advice.

The Spirit of a right Administration must be formed and take its spring from the various parts of the System of the Community and State; from the form and order in which the Individuals within the community, and the Citizens within the State, lie and are distributed. An Administration of Government following these principles, will distinguish the essential unalienable rights of the Individual, both internal, and those which, being external, are communicable, and are melted down into the Communion. It will take care that that full right and

pos-

possession, that free enjoyment of property, which the Individual is entitled to; that those laws of nature which even the establishment of Civil Polity does not interfere in, and which, therefore, remain in the right of the Individual, are not clogged, abated, or obstructed, by any of those perverted conditions which the Governments of the *Old World* have too generally adopted.

The Spirit of the American will, as it hath done, continue to provide for a full, equal, unobstructed, adequate Representation, actuating both Debate and Result, by which the wisdom of the General Community may be concentred; by which the Sense, both in consent and dissent, of the whole, may be regularly collected. It will always provide, as it hath done, for an uniform equable rotation of Obedience and Command.—
" *Neque solum iis præscribendus est Imperandi, sed etiam Civibus obtemperandi Modus. Nam et qui benè imperat, paruerit aliquando necesse est; et qui modestè paret, videbatur, qui aliquando imperet, dignus esse,*

esse. Itaq; oportet ut eum, qui paret, sperare se aliquo tempore imperaturum; et illum, qui imperat, cogitare brevi tempore sibi esse parendum." Cicero de Legibus, Lib. iii. § 2.

This measure of Rotation of Office, and responsibility at the going out of Office, is of the essence of a real Republic.

The State arising from, and being built up in, that Spirit of genuine Liberty, which animates the New World, not in the partial political one of the Old World, which hath a thousand distinctions and exclusions of Nations, Provinces, even Colours of the human Species; the UNITED STATES AND CITIZENS of America, whose System is founded on a Law of Nations that coincides with the Law of Nature, will find it just and right, true in politics, to institute some mode, by which the *Slaves*, whom Providence hath suffered to come under their domination, may work out, by proper means and in suitable time, their Liberty; by means which may not injure the property of the Master-owners, and which may

render

render the Slaves better and more zealous servants, while their Slavery remains. These unhappy People, emerging to liberty, under certain limitations, will become, what the American community most wants, a beneficial Supply of Labourers, Farmers, upon rent, Mechanics and Manufacturers. Perhaps, in order to throw them into these classes, as well as for other reasons, it may be thought one of the proper limitations, to exclude the coloured *Liberti* from a capacity of having or holding any landed Property, other than as Tenants. The Memorialist has his ideas as to the means of carrying this measure into execution. If the States should disapprove the measure itself, the mention of them would become improper. If it should please God to put it into their hearts, to reason, that, while they feel their obligations to his Providence for establishment of their own liberty, they ought to think it a duty required of them to open and extend this blessing to their fellow creatures;

tures; they would be masters of much better ways and means than the Memorialist could suggest, each State adopting by their own legislature such as were suited to their respective peculiar circumstances.

As the UNITED STATES in the New World have no landed Clergy, *no Church Establishment*, as the Religion of the State or the General Government; and as this is a matter so foreign and incomprehensible to common Politicians of the Old World; more than ordinary attention becomes due to the grounds of the Sanction of Oaths. It will be wise to review the Institutions by which Oaths are applied to the interior proceedings of Government; it will be necessary that Foreign powers should understand the Grounds of these Sanctions, both divine and human, by which the obligation of oaths in America stands bound and devoted.

Although the *Modes* of Faith, and Fashions of Ceremonies in the Religion of America, are left as indifferent and irrelevant,

irrelevant, either to the true Essence of Religion, or to the Constitution of the State; yet there is no Country or Region on the Earth, where a real sincere conscientious sense of the divine truths respecting the Supreme Being, and the dispensations of his providence here, and in a future State of Rewards and punishments, are in Spirit and truth so generally impressed on the mind and Character of the Inhabitants; and the States, each within its own jurisdiction, do require of every Citizen, * upon the same Principles

---

* It may not be amiss to give an instance or two of this: first, as it was conceived by those States of the Old World who were under the darkness of the False Religion; and, next, of the general manner in which the American States take up this necessary claim on their Citizens.—*Si igitur hoc a principio persuasum Civibus, Dominos esse omnium rerum ac moderatores Deos : eaq; quæ gerantur eorum geri ditione, ac numine, eosdemq optimè de genere hominum mereri : et Qualis quisq; sit, quid agat, quid in se admittat, quâ mente, quâ pietate colat religiones, intueri, piorumq; etim piorum habere rationem.*——— *Utiles esse autem opiniones has, quis neget, cum intelligat quam multa firmentur jurejurando ; Quantæ Salutis sint Fœderum religiones ; quam multos divini supplicii metus à scelere revocârit, quamq; sancta sit Societas*

ciples that all other States have done, some open testimony and overt act of his religious character. There is, therefore, the same grounds of the Sanction of an oath in the mind and conscience of man towards God, in America, as in any other Country; and, indeed, ground more assuredly to be rested upon, where the religion, being that of the mind and heart, is free in Spirit and Truth, than where it is made

Societas civium inter ipsos, Diis immortalibus interpositis tum Judicibus tum Testibus.—*Cicero* de Repub. L. ii. § 7.

See next how the States of America take up this idea, and make it one of the fundamentals of their System. I will take my instance from the State Massachusett's bay; which shows, that, although that Commonwealth admits no Church establishment, yet it considers Religion as the fundamental principle of a State.——" It is right, as well as the Duty of all Men *in Society*, publicly and at stated seasons to worship the Supreme Being.——As *the happiness of a people*, and *the good order and preservation of the Civil Government*, essentially depend upon Piety, Religion, and Morality; and as these cannot be generally diffused through a Community, but by the Institution of the Public Worship of God, and of public instructions in piety, Religion, and morality; therefore, to promote their happiness, and to secure the good order and preservation of their Government, the People of this Commonwealth

made up of externals forced by eftablifh-ment into practice, which becomes little better than either mechanical habit, or hypocrify. Again; where Men accuftom themfelves to ufe in common converfation the *forms* of oaths by appeals to God, for the truth of their Conduct or of their

affe-

wealth have a right to inveft their Legiflature with power to authorife and require, and the Legiflature fhall, from time to time, authorife and require, the feveral Towns, Parifhes, Precincts, and other Bodies politic, or religious Societies, to make fuitable provifion, at their own expence, for the inftitution of the public worfhip of God, and for the fupport and maintenance of public Proteftant Teachers of Piety, Religion, and Morality, in all cafes where fuch provifion fhall not be made voluntarily.'

'And the People have a right to (and do) inveft their Legiflature with authority to enjoin upon All the Subjects an attendance upon the Inftructions of public Teachers as aforefaid, at ftated times and feafons, if there be any on whofe inftructions they can confcientioufly and conveniently attend.'

'Provided, notwithftanding, that the feveral Towns, Parifhes, Precincts, and other Bodies politic, or religious Societies, fhall at all times have the exclufive right of electing their public teachers, and of contracting with them for their fupport and maintenance.'

'And all monies paid by the Subject to the fupport of public Worfhip, and of the public teachings aforefaid, fhall, if he [that is, any Individual, or

Q.   number

asseverations; or where, in the like profane habit, they do, as it were by a kind of *votive ordeal,* call down upon themselves the vengeance and the curses which God is supposed to pour down on the heads of the perjured: in such countries, and with such habits and characters, there will not be that religious Sense of the solemn Sanction of an oath, as in America, where this profane habit hath not yet pervaded the general manners of the people.

An Oath is, as Cicero * defines it, *Affirmatio religiosa,* Deo *teste.* This being

---

number of Individuals] requires it, be uniformly applied to the support of the public Teacher or Teachers of his own religious Sect or denomination, provided there be any on whose instructions he attends; otherwise it may be paid towards the support of the Teacher or Teachers of the Parish or Precinct in which the said monies are raised.'

'And every Denomination of Christians, demeaning themselves peaceably, and as good subjects of the Commonwealth, shall be equally under the protection of the Law; and no subordination of any one sect to another shall ever be established by Law."
—This Institution, mutatis mutandis, will suit the religious part of every state in America.

* De Off. Lib. iii. § 29.

so solemn an appeal to religion as ought not to be permitted to be violated without the temporal resentment of Civil Society; all States have annexed severe temporal pains and penalties to this daring breach of faith, pledged under the witnessing Eye and Sanction of Heaven. The Sanctions of an Oath are by these means of two kinds: Perjurii pœna *Divina* Exitium; *Humana* Dedecus. Cicero de Leg. Lib. ii. § 9.

If there is not in a People a conscientious habitual sense of the superintending Providence of the Supreme Being, the pœna *Divina*, with the Man or Men who want this Sense of duty towards God, will become a mockery and an ensnaring false pretence to confidence; and the adding an oath, under this callous State of conscience, must operate as such a snare, without insuring truth or right. Nay, even further; where the proper sense of religion remains, if the divine Sanction of Oaths is applied in trivial cases, or too presumptuously

presumptuously recurred to in matters of doubtful temptation, or even made too common on more serious occasions—or is tendered as a form of course in the ordinary occurrences of business,—it will become prophaned; first neglected, and finally contemned. This Error hath been invariably fallen into by all the Governments of the Old World, hath invariably produced the same evil, hath been felt in all, complained of, but never redressed.

It is a common and repeated remark with Historians, when they compare the corruptions of later with the purity of former times, to mark this loss of the *Divine* Sanction of oaths. * Livy, speaking of a transaction, wherein the Tribunes aimed, by a casuistical distinction, to absolve the people from their oaths, says, *Sed nondum hæc, quæ nunc tenet Sæcula, negligentia Deûm venerat, nec interpretando sibi, Quisq; jusjurandum & Leges aptos faciebat, sed suos potiùs mores ad ea accommodat.*

* Lib. iii. § 20.

commodat. The Memorial here recurring to its leading propofition, That, as the Americans are founded on, and *built up in, quite a new Syftem in a New World,* by themfelves, are not only at liberty, but, in the natural courfe of their operations, muft be led to take their meafures from nature and truth, and not from prejudged precedents; whatever inftitutions they form on any new matter or occafion will be original: on this pofition, the Memorialift ventures to proceed in the following reafoning. As the fanctions of an oath are of two kinds, if the oath is tendered and taken under one only of thefe fanctions, the *Pæna,* as Cicero defcribes it, will have a very different reference to the avenging juftice of Heaven, or to the pains and penalties of the Civil Power. The American Legiflators may, perhaps, making this diftinction, be led to feparate thefe two very different forts of Oaths; the Oath taken under the Civil Sanction and Penalties only, from that in which the Divine

vine and Human Sanctions are combined. An oath taken and made, not invoking the presence and attestation of God, but in presence of and pledged to the Civil Magistrate only, under all the pains and penalties of perjury, and, under the Sanction of those penalties, in case of perjury, of being rendered incapable of giving testimony, of doing any act, or enjoying any right, privilege, or thing, which requires the intervention of an Oath, may be sufficient bond of faith in all ordinary cases, in all Forensic or Commerical transactions. *The* OATH *of the higher and more solemn form,* where God is invoked as a witness, wherein he is appealed to as a Judge, and as the direct avenger of perjury; this solemn Oath, in which the Divine Sanction hath also the temporal human Sanction combined with it, should be reserved solely to the most important occasions of the State, either in its Fecial and Foederal transactions with Foreign Nations; or where, within their own System,

tem, the Majesty of the People; the Sovereignty of the State; the vitality of the Constitution; or the life of man is concerned. In the tender and taking of this oath of the higher and solemn sanction, every ceremony, every solemnity, should be used that can tend to impress a right Sense of the Sacred Sanctions under which it is taken.

An institution of this kind, planned and formed by the wisdom of the Assemblies of the States, with all the provisions, distinctions, and limitations, which they will best know how to apply, would avoid all those evils arising from the defect or corruption of the divine sanction of oaths; would preserve more sacred that sanction; and maintain its operative effect on the minds of men longer than any State of the Old World hath been able ever yet to do.

This Memorial doth not presume to review the establishment of the Military Part of the States; nor the form under which

which the Continental Army was constituted: if it did, it could be only to say, that nothing could be better calculated, nothing more wisely grounded, so as to harrass the people as little as possible, and yet always to be in practical promptitude, and efficiency, to execute the very service for which it was called forth.

It declines, also, saying any thing on the Naval Department, as that subject seems to the Memorialist to require the discussion of a previous question, of great import either way, and a matter of deep policy, of which the Memorialist is not competent to judge; namely, whether that Force should be brought forward into force equal to the capabilities of the Empire, *all at once*, by one great united effort; or be let to grow by a natural successive progression in the ordinary train of affairs?

There are one or two points which lie not, indeed, so much in matter of Administration, as in the procedure of executive Justice.

The

The first is the new mode by which the States and the General Government must define and clafs the Crime of Treafon, and Offences againft the *Majeftas* and the *Salus Populi*, and the Sovereignty of the State. The Governments of the latter periods of the Old World being Feudal, and there being no idea of Sovereignty but of that which was Perfonal, the Crime of Treafon was confined to overt acts committed againft this Perfonal Sovereign: but in the new Syftem and Conftitution of the UNITED STATES, the object *is the State, not the Perfon.* This Crime muft be defcribed, defined, and claffed under its feveral degrees of criminality, according to this latter Idea. Here the Wifdom of Congrefs and of the States cannot act too much upon caution, cannot too attentively, too anxioufly, apply that caution, to guard itfelf againft the errors into which the Romans were betrayed, and which, under this law of *læfa Majeftas*, gave fcope to the moft cruel engine of Tyranny.

There are not, nor ever were, in America, any of those *Forest-laws*, if Laws they can be called, which were the mere denunciations of Tyranny and Domination; Regulations that ruined the poor subjects of the Monarchs of Europe, in order to insure the preservation of their beasts of the Chace. This tyranny became intolerable every where; in Britain it was wrenched out of the hands of the Monarch. If the suppression of this domination had been made under the genuine Spirit of Liberty, the mischief would have ended here; but a hundred heads of petty Tyrants sprung out of the neck of this Hydra principle. A System of *Game-Laws* became established in the hands of lesser, but more mischievous Tyrants; and in their hands became snares round the necks, and as whips of scorpions over the backs of the lesser inhabitants of the land, the unqualified Yeomanry and Tenantry: but the Spirit of America revolts against such baseness; the very air will not permit it; what is *Wild by Nature*

Nature is there Game to every Individual, who is *free by nature*. There are laws to secure to each land-holder, the quiet enjoyment of his land against real trespass and damage; but there are no *Game-laws* in America: that impudent Tyranny hath not yet, and, I trust, never will, dare to show its head in that Land of Liberty.

There is another matter of Police, which being, as the Memorialist conceives, an almost general Error of the Governments of the Old World, and such as he thinks the System and Principles of the New World will reform, he will not pass by in silence. He thinks that *imprisonment for debt* is a direct solecism in policy, not relevant to the ends of distributive Justice, and contrary to every idea of the advantages which the Community is supposed to derive, in some degree or other, from every individual. Imprisonment cannot pay the debt; is a punishment that makes no distinction between criminality, or the misfortune, which may have occafioned the debt. The glaring injuftice of this punifhment hath led to two remedial Laws, the Statutes of Bankruptcy and Statutes of Infolvency, which are fources of endlefs frauds. The locking-up the debtor from all means of Labour or Employment, is robbing the community of the profit of that labour or employment which might be produced, and is making the Debtor a burthen to his Creditor and to the public. If any fraud or other criminality appears amongft the caufes of the debt; or if it hath been occafioned by an undue courfe of living above the circumftances of the debtor; correct the vicious Follies, punifh the Fraud. But taking the Debtor, fimply as a debtor, pity his misfortune; do juftice, neverthelefs, to the Creditor. Inftead of fhutting the man up from all means of maintenance, * indent

---

* This Indenting of a Servant for a number of years, three, four, or feven, as the Europeans do apprentices, is a practice of every day: where New-comers into the Country,—fome poffeffing large fums, indent

dent him to his Creditor or Creditors as a bond servant; or where misfortune and not criminality, put him in some or other way by which some profit may be drawn from him. If he cannot labour in one way, he may be employed in another; for when obliged to it he will become useful in some way or other. If his mode of labour or capacity for employment be not of immediate use to his creditor, that creditor can sell his time to some other person, to whom it may become so; the Creditor will thus, in part, be reimbursed; the profit (how small is not here the consideration) will not be lost to the Community; and the dread of being reduced to this servile state will be a greater terror to debtors becoming so by fraud and criminality, than any confinement in any jail whatsoever.

The Americans will excuse the Memorialist, if he mentions one matter more;

---

dent themselves as Servants for three or four years, in order to learn the business of the Country before they settle in its Lands.

which

which is, a caution againſt their falling into that falſe police of the Old World which hath manacled the hands of Labour, and puts fetters on the activity of the Human Being; which hath fixed him to one Spot, and, as it were, to a vegetable mechaniſm, whom Nature meant ſhould be locomotive, ſeeking his means of labour and employ where he could beſt profit of his powers and capacities. He mentions this as a guard againſt their interfering with the free courſe of Labour; the free employment of Stock, either by direct regulating and prohibitory laws; by partial privileges, on one hand, or checks on the other; or by any local or perſonal privileges, which is a bounty on idleneſs, and deſtroys all competition; or by fooliſh bounties, which put every account of manufactures or commerce on a falſe balance at the outſet, which is never after ſet right. He hopes the Americans will excuſe this exceſs of caution in an European, who has ſeen the evil effects of all theſe errors in police. He knows that

there

there is no such Spirit of Police in America, and he thinks he may hope there never will be.

Having thus discussed the *Essence* of the New System in the New World; the genuine Spirit of Liberty which animates it ; the Spirit of Sovereignty that actuates it ; the *equal temper* of a community of Equals which gives equable and uniform motion to it : having examined those relative matters which may, both internally and externally, affect the *existence* of this independent Sovereign; those points more particularly which are necessary to give it Efficiency, and to assure its Permanency: Having, by a concurrent analysis of its actual Situation with the Principles of the System, shewn how the Constitution is is founded on nature, and built up in Truth ; having explained (according to the manner in which the Memorialist reasons) how some new and original institutions of Policy ought to arise out of it : having marked what ought to be, and

what

what will be, *the Reason of State, the Spirit of Administration* of such a free Sovereign, so founded and so built up: The Memorial will now venture, in the words of the Prophet*, for this Prophet was as true a Patriot, as deep a Politician, as he was a sound Divine, to say to the Sovereign Government of America,

1. Arise, ascend thy Lofty Seat.
2. Be cloathed with thy Strength.
3. Lift up on high a Standard to the Nations.

Actuate your Sovereignty: exercise the powers and Duties of your Throne. Let the Supream Magistrate or Magistrates be visibly *cloathed* with the Majesty of the People; and seen to be armed with the efficient powers of Administration; and constantly attended with the rewards and Punishments of executive Justice. The Magistrate or Magistrates should not only have all those powers, but *be cloathed*

* Isaiah.

with

with them, as with a Robe of State. The Fasces or other Insignia Juris et Majestatis Imperii should precede this Magistracy in some visible form, whenever he or they come forth in the forms of office. These are expressed by the *Insignia* and *Fasces* which the Romans fixt in attendance on the Consuls, after they had abolished the pomp and parade of their King.

It is not sufficient that the United States feel that they are Sovereign; it is not sufficient that the sense of this is universally felt in America; it is not sufficient that they are conscious to themselves that the *Punctum Saliens,* the Source and Spring of the Activity of this Sovereign power, is within their System: until they *lift up on high a Standard to the Nations,* it will remain as an abstract idea, as a Theory in the World at large. This Sovereign must come forward amongst the Nations, as an active Existing Agent, a Personal Being, standing on the same ground as all other Personal Sovereigns.

Its Powers, Commissions, Officers Civil and Military; its claims to, and its exercise of, the Rights of the Law of Nations, must have their full and free scope in act and deed: wherever they come forward, their Standard and Flag, the Ensign of the Majesty of their Sovereignty, must be erected; and its rights and privileges established amongst the Nations of the Earth; it must be acknowledged; respected; and, in all cases whatsoever, *treated as what it is*, the Actual Signal of a Sovereign Empire.

The Supream * Magistrate of this confederate State when placed on the Throne of Empire, will become animated, and feel himself actuated by a sense of Sovereign power; of his being the administering Officer of a Free People: and the People, conscious that they are mutually

---

* I here use the word Magistrate singularly, as meaning Magistracy, instead of repeatedly using the expression Magistrate or Magistrates.

Participants, and in common Constituent-Members, of this Sovereignty, will feel a reciprocal sense of the Duty of Obedience.

The Popular Branch of a State, the People, are always found attached to their ancient Government; the Allegiance is so worn into habit, as to create a home-sense of its being *Their own Government*: this is an artificial conscience, an acquired opinion, a secondary principle. But when a People feel, that this Government is of their own establishment and Structure; that the Magistrate administering is of their own creation; and that each one of themselves is capable in rotation of becoming that Magistrate; they feel directly, primarily, on the fact, that this Government is their own *Imperium*, and the Duty of Obedience operates as by a sense of Nature.

The Supream Magistrate of this Republic will feel, that the Community meant that the Sovereignty should be Efficient; and that He is entrusted by the Confidence

Confidence of the People so to actuate it. He will assume to his Character this confidence. He will have the consciousness of knowing that He is the actuating spirit of the concentred Vitality of the State; and that His first and direct duty is the preservation thereof in all its functions, health, and efficiency. He ought to fear nothing so much as the doing or suffering any thing that may hurt the *Salus Reipub.* that may diminish or abate the Majesty of the People. It is not sufficient that his office and Character have respect annexed to them; but He ought to acquire an Ascendency that will command respect. He ought to be cloathed with the palpable visible Authority and Power of the *Imperium.* He ought to stand above the level of Equality; He ought, wherever he is seen, to impress a sense and an idea of Superiority and Eminence; He ought to be looked up to as the shield of the Good, and as the armed avenging hand of Evil. The People ought to see, (and, if the conſtitution of the State be conform to the Syſtem of the Community, they will ſee,) that, as all political information centers in this office; as the Wiſdom of the State is concentred there; ſo the Activity of the State ſprings from it. Thus Seated on the Throne of Empire, the Supreme Magiſtrate of a State formed of a Free People, where the intereſt of the Rulers and of the People coincide, or rather are the ſame; the People and the Rulers cannot have two different views of things; the Rulers can have no Intereſt, no Wiſh, to repreſent or to treat things different from what they are. In a State ſo conſtituted and ſo arranged in its adminiſtration, there cannot be even a temptation to deceive on the part of the Rulers; there cannot be any ground to ſuſpect ſuch on the part of the People. It is only when the Government is built up contrary to the fundamental Syſtem of the Community, or, being perverted, becomes ſo,

that

that deceit, corruption, or violence, can become a meaſure of State Policy. In a real Republic, which is *Res Populi*, the Proceſſion of its conſtitution, and the courſe of its actions, ariſe from Nature and Truth; all Deception, all Corrupt influence, all Violence, is directly contrary to the true principles of politics. Without Truth and Juſtice, a Republic cannot be adminiſtered or governed. The Supream Magiſtrate of ſuch a free State, muſt, from the nature of his information, ſee things as they lie in Nature, and will of Courſe found his Meaſures in Truth. Truth is not only a virtue, but is Wiſdom; and, in a government of a real Republic, ſuch as the Empire of America, is the only Genuine Policy. It creates truſt, finds Union and Confidence. And, laſtly, an Adminiſtration actuated by ſuch principles and maxims, finds itſelf *Cloathea with Strength*, the united ſtrength of the Peo-

People *. Where there is a right knowledge in a Supream Magistrate of the Duty of administering a Republic, that Magistrate will be above all wretched King-craft and Cunning. Such is only necessary to false Power, to half spirit, and half sense. The Magistrate who acts with real power, and understands his own situation and duty, will treat Persons and Things *as what they are:* he knows exactly the line and takes it, and discerns of course the crooked one, only to avoid it. Truth has but one plain road to take; it is open, and is the best Policy. As it

* This is not vision, such as the Statesmen of Europe, who are wise in their Generation of Corruption, may call it: it is Fact. And the Memorialist feels a conscious pride that He dare appeal to the State Massachusett's-bay, for an Example, in a period wherein the Rulers and the People had but one View of things, but one line of Conduct; wherein more real Exertions were made for the Public Service, than in any other Period, wherein the People have been attempted to be ruled by *the Art of Governing*, by deception, by corrupt influence, by violence.

doth

doth itself command Nature; it will lead a Republic to command to the utmost extent of its Capacities and Powers.

That Spirit of Uniform Justice, *quæ nec puniendo irritat animum immanem; nec omnia prætermittendo, licentiâ, Cives deteriores reddit*, is inseparably allied to this of Truth.

The Spirit of Magnanimity, that Spirit which never ceases to feel that it is acting the part of a Sovereign over a Free People, who Governs by Authority within the State, and holds up his head with an ascendant address amongst his Equals, other Sovereigns of the Earth, is another constituent part of this character.

A temper of invariable universal Benevolence, which circumscribes all the rest, and binds the Character into perfect System, is the crown of these (I will call them) political virtues.

Being thus planted in a New System in a New Country; growing up under such
prin-

principles of Truth and Nature; established in such a Constitution of Government; having in so short a period been brought forward to Independence, and become Sovereigns acknowledged so by the Sovereigns of Europe; all this coming into Event by Something beyond the ordinary course of Events in human affairs, THE UNITED STATES AND CITIZENS OF AMERICA may say, " *It is the Lord's* " *doings.*" But let them remember, that enjoying a System of police that gives activity to their powers; that inhabiting a New World, a land of plenty and liberty; a country which hath so many sources of enjoyments which it offers to the Old World—let them remember the obligations which Heaven hath thus laid on them, and the returns which this Goodness reclaims of them; that They respect the rights and liberties of Mankind; that by a free commerce they diffuse to the World at large the surplus portion of these

T good

good things which they muſt be continually creating in their own World; that they conſider themſelves as the means in the hands of Providence, of extending the Civilization of human Society; and the Teachers, by their example, of thoſe Political Truths, which are meant, not to enſlave, but to render men more free and happy under Government.—If they take up this Character within themſelves, and hold out its operations and effect to the Old World, they will become a Nation *to whom all Nations will come*; a Power whom all the Powers of Europe will court to Civil and Commercial Alliances; a People to whom the Remnants of all ruined People will fly, whom all the oppreſſed and injured of every nation will ſeek to for refuge. *The riches of the Sea will pour in upon them; the wealth of Nations muſt flow in upon them;* and they muſt be a populous and Rich People.

That all this, UNITED STATES AND CITI-

Citizens of America, may tend to your own real Good, Peace, and Liberty; that all this may prove the natural means, under the bleſſings of Heaven, of General Liberty, Peace, and Happineſs to Mankind, as the utmoſt that Human Nature here on earth can look to, is the ardent wiſh and anxious prayer of Your Memorialiſt

T. POWNALL.

FINIS

New Publications printed for J. Debrett, (Successor to Mr. Almon,) opposite Burlington-House, Piccadilly.

A MEMORIAL, humbly addressed to the SOVEREIGNS of EUROPE. Second Edition. By Thomas Pownall, Esq. Price 2s. 6d.

THE PARLIAMENTARY REGISTER. Containing the most full and accurate Account of the Debates and Proceedings of both Houses of Parliament, from the general Election in 1774, to the Dissolution in 1780. In seventeen volumes, Price 6l. 6s. half-bound and lettered.

The PARLIAMENTARY REGISTER of the FIRST and SECOND SESSIONS of the 15th Parliament of Great-Britain, 8 vols. Price Three Guineas half-bound and lettered.

** This work has been honoured with the approbation and assistance of many of the first persons in this country; nor has the encouragement given to this work by the public been a less honourable testimony of their approbation also. Flattered by these rewards, the editors have never hesitated at any expence in procuring authentic copies of all important papers that might enrich the work, and render it worthy of the public patronage.

The REMEMBRANCER, or Impartial Repository of Public Events. Published monthly. Price 1s. each number.

The war in America suggested the utility of a periodical collection of the best accounts of every important public transaction. The work commenced in June, 1775, in England; authentic paper, whether published in America, by the British Ministry, or the Congress; the letters of the several Officers; addresses, resolutions, of Committees, Conventions, the Continental Congress, &c. &c. are all carefully inserted in it; together with many interesting papers upon other subjects. The price of the 17 volumes, half-bound and lettered, is 5l. 12s.

A Collection of STATE PAPERS, relative to the FIRST Acknowledgment of the INDEPENDENCY of the United States of North America, by their High Mightinesses the States General of the United Netherlands; to which is prefixed, the Political Character of JOHN ADAMS, Esq. Ambassador Plenipotentiary from the States of North-America, &c. Price 2s.

NEW PUBLICATIONS,

Printed for J. DEBRETT, (Succeſſor to Mr. ALMON) oppoſite Burlington-Houſe, Piccadilly.

THE PARLIAMENTARY REGISTER, No. X. of the preſent Seſſion, and LXVIII. from the laſt General Election; price 1s. each. This Work contains, beſides the fulleſt and moſt impartial Report of the DEBATES and PROCEEDINGS in both Houſes of PARLIAMENT, authentic Copies of all IMPORTANT Papers laid upon the Table of either Houſe, thereby furniſhing to the Members themſelves eſſential Matters not in the Votes or Journals, and to the Public at large, a thorough and complete Knowledge of all Documents and Proceeding of Parliament.

Of whom may be had, The PARLIAMENTARY REGISTER of the laſt Parliament, from the General Election in 1774, to the Diſſolution in 1780, in Seventeen Volumes, half-bound and lettered, Price Six Guineas. The Firſt and Second Seſſion of the preſent Parliament, in Eight Volumes, half-bound and lettered, price 3l. 3s.

The REMEMBRANCER; or IMPARTIAL REPOSITORY of PUBLIC EVENTS. Price 1s. each Number.—The AMERICAN WAR gave riſe to this Work in 1775. Every authentic Paper relative to that War, as alſo with France and Spain, whether publiſhed in ENGLAND, or AMERICA, by the BRITISH MINISTRY, or the AMERICAN CONGRESS, are all carefully inſerted in this Work. The Letters of the ſeveral Commanding Officers, Addreſſes, Reſolutions of the various Committees, Conventions, &c. Complete Sets of this valuable and intereſting Work may be had of the Publiſher in Sixteen Volumes. Price 5l. 5s. half-bound and lettered.

THE NARRATIVE of Lieutenant General Sir HENRY CLINTON, K. B. relative to his Conduct during Part of his Command of the King's Troops in North America: particularly to that which reſpects the unfortunate Iſſue of the Campaign in 1781. Sixth Edition. Price 2s

AN ANSWER to That Part of the Narrative of Lieut. Gen. Sir HENRY CLINTON, K. B. which relates to the Conduct of Lieut. General Earl Cornwallis during the Campaign in North America, in the year 1781, by Earl Cornwallis. Price 3s. ſewed.

OBSERVATIONS upon ſome parts of Lieutenant General EARL CORNWALLIS's ANSWER to Sir HENRY CLINTON's Narrative. By Lieutenant-General Sir HENRY CLINTON, K. B. Price 2s. 6d. The above three authentic publications comprehend the Whole of this very intereſting controverſy, and being all uniformly printed, may be had complete in One Volume. Price 8s. half-bound and lettered.

GENERAL BURGOYNE's STATE of his EXPEDITION from CANADA, with all the authentic Documents, and many Circumſtances not made public before. Written by himſelf. Illuſtrated

NEW PUBLICATIONS.

trated with six Plans of the Action, the Country, &c. finely engraved and coloured. A new Edition, in Octavo. Price 6s. in Boards.

Sir WILLIAM HOWE's NARRATIVE, relative to his Conduct during his late Command of the King's Troops in North America. Third Edition. Price 3s.

A candid and Impartial NARRATIVE of the Transactions of the Fleet under the Command of LORD VISCOUNT HOWE, from the Arrival of the Toulon Squadron on the Coast of America, to the Time of his Lordship's Departure for England. Second Edition. Price 1s. 6d.

BLAKE's REMARKS on Commodore Johnstone's Account of his Engagement with Monsieur de Suffrein, a new Edition; to which is prefixed a Plan of the Harbour, with the Soundings, &c. drawn on the Spot. Price 1s.

THOUGHTS on the CONSTITUTION with a View to the proposed Representation of the People and Duration of Parliaments, by *Lord Carysfort*. Price 1s. 6d.

OBSERVATIONS on the Honourable Lieutenant General MURRAY's Defence by Lieutenant General Sir *William Draper*, K. B. Price 1s. 6d.

NARRATIVE of the late Transactions at Benares, by the Honourable Warren Hastings, Esq. Governor General of Bengal.

EXTRACT of an ORIGINAL LETTER from CALCUTTA, relative to the Administration of Justice, by Sir Elijah Impey. Price 1s. 6d.

ORIGINAL MINUTES of the GOVERNOR GENERAL and COUNCIL of FORT WILLIAM on the Settlement, and Collection of the Revenues of Bengal: with a Plan of Settlement recommended to the Court of Directors, by *Philip Francis*, Esq. Price 7s. 6d. in Boards.

TRAVELLING ANECDOTES through various Parts of EUROPE, Volume I. illustrated with Plates. Price 6s. in Boards.

THOUGHTS on HUNTING, in a Series of Letters by Peter Beckford, Esq. illustrated with an elegant Frontispiece, designed by Cipriani, and engraved by Bartolozzi. Price 7s. 6d. in Boards.

A DEFENCE of the Right Hon. the Earl of Shelburne, from the Reproaches of his numerous Enemies; in a Letter to Sir George Savile, Bart. to which is added, a Postscript, addressed to the Right Honourable John Earl of Stair. Ninth Edition. Price 1s. 6d.

REMARKS upon the Report of a Peace, in Consequence of Mr. Secretary Townshend's Letter to the Lord Mayor of London, Bank Directors, &c. By the Author of the Defence of the Earl of Shelburne. Third Edition. Price 1s.

A LETTER to the First Belfast Company of Volunteers, in the Province of Ulster. By a Member of the British Parliament. Third Edition. Price 1s. 6d.

A LETTER

NEW PUBLICATIONS.

A LETTER to Lord Viscount Beauchamp, upon the Subject of his Letter to the First Belfast Company of Volunteers in the Province of Ulster. Price 1s.

A WORD at PARTING; to the Earl of Shelburne. Price 1s.

AN INQUIRY into the Manners, Taste, and Amusements, of the two last Centuries in England. By John Andrews, LL. D. Price 2s. 6d. sewed.

AN ANSWER to the Disquisition on Government and Civil Liberty, in a Letter to the Author of Disquisitions on several Subjects. Price 1s.

The SPEECH of the Right Hon. Charles James Fox, at a General Meeting of the Electors of Westminster, assembled in Westminster-Hall, July 17, 1782. Taken in Short Hand, by Mr. Blanchard. Illustrated with an elegant and correct Likeness of the Right Honourable Mr. Fox. Price 1s.

A LETTER to the Earl of Shelburne, on the Subject of Mr. Secretary Townshend's Letter to the Chairman of the India Company. Price 6d.

A Collection of STATE PAPERS, relative to the First Acknowledgement of the Independency of the United States of North America, by their High Mightinesses the States General of the United Netherlands. Price 2s.

A SERIOUS ADDRESS to the Electors of Great Britain, on the Subject of Short Parliaments, and an equal Representation.

AN ADDRESS to the People of England, on the intended REFORMATION of PARLIAMENT, price 1s.

LUCUBRATIONS by John Sinclair, Esq. M. P. containing a Plan for a more equal Representation of the People. A new Edition, price 1s. 6d.

A REVIEW of Mrs. SIDDONS and Mrs. CRAWFORD, in the Character of BELVIDERA; third Edition, price 1s. 6d.

ADDRESS to the Right Honourable Henry Grattan, from the Independent Dublin Volunteers, relative to the simple Repeal and the recent Interference of the Earl of Mansfield, &c. price 1s.

A LETTER to RICHARD HILL, Esq. Member for the County of Salop: Author of the Sky-Rocket, Tables Turned, &c. by a Freeholder, 3d Edition, price 1s. 6d.

A SEAMAN's REMARKS on the British Ships of the Line, from the 1st of January 1756, to the 1st of January 1782, with some occasional Observations on the Fleets of the House of Bourbon, price 6d.

COMMON SENSE; addressed to the Inhabitants of America, on a Variety of interesting Subjects. By Thomas Paine, M. A. of the University of Pennsylvania, Author of the Letter to the Abbé Raynal, on the Affairs of North America.

The EARL of ABINGDON's Two late Speeches in the House of Lords, with his Lordship's celebrated Bill on the Occasion, price 6d.

An ESSAY on the NATURE of a LOAN, being an Introduction to the Knowledge of the Public Accounts, price 6d.

NEW PUBLICATIONS.

ORIGINAL Minutes of the Governor General and Council of Bengal, on the Appointment, recommended and carried by Mr. Haftings, in October 1780, of Sir Elijah Impey, to be Judge of Sudder Dewanny Adawlet. Price 1s.

A COMPANION to the ROYAL KALENDAR, for the Year 1783; being a Lift of all the Changes in Adminiftration, from the Acceffion of the pfrefent King, in October 1760, to the prefent Time. To which is prefixed, A lift of the late and prefent Houfe of Commons, fhewing the Changes made in the Members of Parliament, by the General Election in September 1780; with the Names of the Candidates where the Elections were contefted, the Numbers polled, and the Decifions fince made by the Select Committees, &c. The Thirty Second Edition, price 1s.—This Companion is printed in the fame Size as the Royal Kalendar, and they may always be bound together, with or without an Almanack.

A LETTER to the Earl of Shelburne on the Peace. Third Edition. Price 1s.

Authentic Copies of the PRELIMINARY ARTICLES between the Courts of France and Spain, and the PROVISIONAL ARTICLES with the United States of North America. Price 1s.

The Subftance of the Speech of the Right Hon. WILLIAM PITT, on Friday, February 21, 1783. Price 1s.

The DEAN and the 'SQUIRE, a Political Eclogue, humbly dedicated to Soame Jenyns, Efq. by the Author of the Heroic Epiftle to Sir W. CHAMBERS, &c. Price 1s. 6d.—Of whom may be had the Author's Works complete. Price 6s. in Boards.

OBSERVATIONS on the Natural and Civil Rights of Mankind, the Prerogatives of Princes and the Powers of Government, &c. by the Rev. Thomas Northcote, Chaplain in the Royal Artillery, price 1s.

PORTRAITS of the GENERALS, MINISTERS, MAGISTRATES, MEMBERS of CONGRESS, and OTHERS, who have rendered themfelves illuftrious in the Revolution of the UNITED STATES of NORTH AMERICA; drawn from the Life; and engraved by the moft eminent Artifts in London.—— Number I. Price ONE GUINEA, containing the following PORTRAITS. General WASHINGTON, HENRY LAURENS. JOHN JAY, SAM. HUNTINGDON, CHA. THOMSON, JOHN DICKENSON, SILAS DEANE, G. MORRIS, and W. H. DRAYTON, Efqrs. Major General BARON STEUBEN, and Gen. GATES.

OBSERVATIONS on the Commerce of the AMERICAN STATES with EUROPE and the WEST INDIES, including a State of their Imports and Exports. By a MEMBER of PARLIAMENT.

The RESCUE, a Poem, infcribed to the Right Honourable CHARLES JAMES FOX. Price 1s. 6d.

A MEMORIAL, addreffed to the SOVEREIGNS of AMERICA. By T. POWNALL, Efq. late Governor, Captain-General, Vice-Admiral of the Provinces, now STATES, Maffachufetts-Bay, and South-Carolina, and Lieut. Gov. of New-Jerfey

www.ingramcontent.com/pod-product-compliance
Lightning Source LLC
Chambersburg PA
CBHW032113230426
43672CB00009B/1724